Patchwork and Quilting
Book Number 1
Thirteen designs
by KAFFE FASSETT

A WESTMINSTER PRODUCTION

First Published in Great Britain in 1999 by
Rowan Yarns
Green Lane Mill
Holmfirth
West Yorkshire
England
HD7 1RW

Published in the U. S. A. by
Westminster Fibers Inc.
5 Northern Boulevard,
Amherst,
New Hampshire 03031
U. S. A.

Editor and text: Jane Bolsover
Art Director: Kim Hargreaves
Patchwork Designs: Kaffe Fassett
Technical advisors and patchwork assembly: Liza Prior Lucy and Pauline Smith
Photographer: Joey Toller
Liza Prior Lucy photographer: Jack Rosen
Design layout: Les Dunford
Techniques illustrations: Jane Bolsover
Patchwork instruction diagrams: Siriol Clarry
Sub Editor: Natalie Minnis

American Congress Library
Westminster Fibers
Patchwork and Quilting
IBSN 0-9672985-0-4

Color reproduction by Chroma Graphics (Overseas) Pte. Ltd
Printed and bound in Singapore by KHL Printing Co. Pte. Ltd.

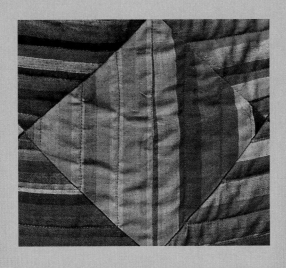

CONTENTS

INTRODUCTION	4	BIOGRAPHIES	20
PATCHWORK IMAGES	5	PATCHWORK AND QUILTING	
Stone Star Bag	5	ASSEMBLY INSTRUCTIONS	21
Striped Triangle Cushion	6	Abbreviations	21
Striped Triangle Quilt	7	Striped Triangle Quilt	22
Pastel Tumbling Blocks Quilt	8	Striped Triangle Cushion	24
Baby Star Quilt	9	Striped Triangle Bag	25
Striped Triangle Bag	10	Big Star Quilt	26
Dark Star Quilt	11	Baby Star Quilt	28
Big Star Quilt	12	Dark Star Quilt	31
Stone Star Cushion	14	Jewel and Stone Star Cushions	33
Ochre Pennants Tablecloth	15	Jewel and Stone Star Bags	34
Jewel Star Bag	16	Magenta Floating Blocks Quilt	35
Magenta Floating Blocks Quilt	17	Ochre Pennants Tablecloth	38
		Pastel Tumbling Blocks Quilt	40
PATCHWORK FLAT SHOTS	18	PATCHWORK KNOW-HOW	43
Pastel Tumbling Blocks Quilt	18		
Ochre Pennants Tablecloth	18	GLOSSARY	47
Dark Star Quilt	18		
Magenta Floating Blocks Quilt	19	TEMPLATES	49
Striped Triangle Quilt	19		
Big Star Quilt	19	INDEX	55

INTRODUCTION

For years I did needlepoint and knitting. Sometimes I still do. These were mostly solitary endeavours. When I began to do patchwork quilting I discovered the unique camaraderie that accompanies this needle art. Women have found themselves sharing their stories around a quilting frame for centuries. I think this is the original 'self-help' therapy group. I have certainly found this companionship in my work with the incredibly generous artist Kaffe Fassett, since we began collaborating on our book, *Glorious Patchwork*. While developing our quilts, we shared our lives, our hopes, our joys, our love of color and textiles – as well as our passion for singing badly out loud!

Others have shared their expertise to help us in this project, including the talented needleworker Pauline Smith. The book could not have been produced without the support and confidence of Stephen Sheard at Rowan and Ken and June Bridgewater of Westminster Fibers, who created the glorious fabrics used in our beautiful patchworks. We are also grateful to Jane Bolsover for her ability to turn our creations into a working manual for you to follow, and to many others who have worked hard to make our book possible. They have all gathered around our quilting frame to share their ideas.

We invite you to join us in using the Kaffe Fassett Striped Fabrics and the Glorious Patchwork Fabric Collection to make the designs within these pages for yourself. And if you ever want to sing badly out loud with a friend while stitching, I can assure you it is a joyous experience!

Liza Prior Lucy

Stone Star Bag

5

Striped Triangle Quilt

Pastel Tumbling Blocks Quilt

8

Baby Star Quilt

Striped Triangle Bag

Dark Star Quilt

Big Star Quilt

Stone Star Cushion

14

Ochre Pennants Tablecloth

Jewel Star Bag

Magenta Floating Blocks Quilt

PATCHWORK FLAT SHOTS

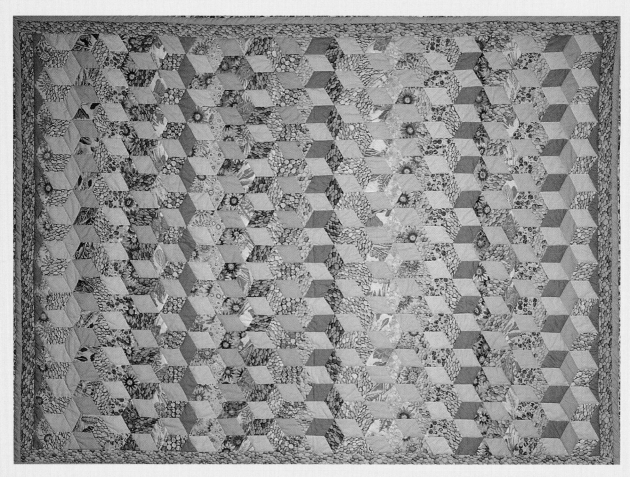

Pastel Tumbling Blocks Quilt   94in x 67½in (240cm x 172cm)

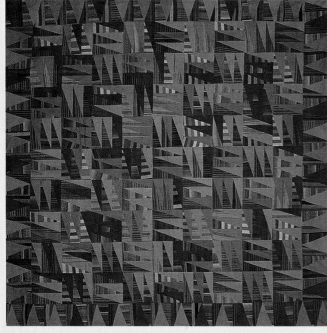

Ochre Pennants Tablecloth
66½in x 66½in (169cm x169cm)

Dark Star Quilt
42in x 40in (106cm x 101cm)

Magenta Floating Blocks Quilt
80in x 55in (203cm x 140cm)

Striped Triangle Quilt
90in x 60in (228cm x 152cm)

Big Star Quilt   94in x 91in (239cm x 230cm)

BIOGRAPHIES

Kaffe Fassett

Born in San Francisco, Kaffe settled in England in 1964, and worked as an artist. On a trip to Scotland he stumbled on an irresistible collection of coloured yarns. A few months later he was hooked and proceeded to knit and stitch himself a career, publishing his first book, *Glorious Knitting*, in 1986. For the last 15 years, Kaffe has worked closely with Rowan Yarns producing ambitious designer patterns to inspire hand knitters world-wide. In 1996 Kaffe was asked by the charity Oxfam to visit poverty stricken weaving villages in India and Guatemala to advise on designs that could be marketed in the west. A wonderful range of striped patchwork fabrics was the result.

After meeting Liza Prior Lucy, she urged him to do a book on her great passion, patchwork. This was the beginning of a new adventure and Kaffe's first patchwork collection was published in 1997: *Glorious Patchwork*.

Pauline Smith

Pauline Smith has been a quiltmaker since her college days, when she trained in Printed Textile Design at Bournemouth & Poole College of Art. It was the cold weather that inspired her to start quilting - as well as a visit to the American Museum in Bath. She made her first quilt by cutting up old clothes. Postgraduate teacher training at Bretton Hall College brought her to Yorkshire in 1969, where she married and now lives.

Pauline built up a successful business designing and making patchwork, which led to her partnership in 'Up Country', a shop whose speciality was textiles and which sold Rowan yarns. Since selling the shop Pauline has been working as a patchwork consultant for Rowan, where she works with Kaffe Fassett. She also holds knitting and embroidery courses at her studio in Oldfield.

Liza Prior Lucy

Liza Prior Lucy first began making quilts in 1990. She was so enthralled by the craftspeople she met and by the generously stocked quilt fabric shops in the States, that quiltmaking soon became a passion. Liza originally trained as a knitwear designer and produced features for needlework magazines. She has also owned and operated her own needlepoint shop in Washington, DC. Liza met Kaffe when she was working as a Sales Representative for Rowan Yarns in the New York City area - Kaffe had come to America to promote his books and was working as Rowan's leading designer. They worked very closely together both in the States and in the UK to write and produce the quilts for the book *Glorious Patchwork*. Liza lives in historic New Hope, Pennsylvania, with her husband Drew, two daughters Alexandra and Elizabeth and the family bulldog, Zoe.

Jane Bolsover

Jane Bolsover has 20 years' experience in the sewing industry and is currently Sewing Editor for the national UK magazine *Essentials*. After training in Fashion and Design in Leicester, Jane worked for a variety of companies over 11 years, and was given the opportunity to collaborate with leading designers of the time, such as Bill Gibb and Benny Ong. Since then, Jane has written articles on sewing and dressmaking for several well-known UK-based magazines, as well as writing the book *Cushions and Covers* for the Country Craft series. Jane has appeared on mainstream television several times, demonstrating her talents with textiles. She is also a regular contributor at major sewing exhibitions and demonstrates for international companies, giving advice on fabric, soft furnishings and general dressmaking. Jane lives in Oxfordshire, England, with her two cats, Chole and Loulou.

Patchwork and Quilting Assembly Instructions

EXPERIENCE RATINGS

Striped Triangle Quilt	★
Striped Triangle Cushion	★
Striped Triangle Bag	★
Big Star Quilt	★★
Baby Star Quilt	★★★
Dark Star Quilt	★★★

Jewel and Stone Star Cushions	★★
Jewel and Stone Star Bags	★★
Magenta Floating Blocks Quilt	★★
Ochre Pennants Tablecloth	★★
Pastel Tumbling Blocks Quilt	★★★

Key

★ = Easy, straightforward, suitable for a beginner.
★★ = Suitable for the average patchworker and quilter.
★★★ = For the more experienced patchworker and quilter.

ABBREVIATIONS

The Kaffe Fassett Fabric collection

Prints			Print colour codes			Stripes		
GP06	=	Pebble Beach	L	=	leafy	NS	=	Narrow stripe
GP01	=	Roman Glass	J	=	jewel	PS	=	Pachrangi stripe
GP03	=	Gazania	S	=	stone	ES	=	Exotic stripe
GP09	=	Chard	C	=	circus	AS	=	Alternate stripe
GP04	=	Beads	P	=	pastel	BS	=	Broad stripe

The Kaffe Fassett fabrics are available at Rowan stockists in Europe and the Far East. In U.S.A., Canada and Australasia they are available through Westminster stockists and better fabric stores.

Plain fabrics

(Not in Rowan or Westminster collections)

PBL	=	pale blue	LC	=	lilac	TE	=	terracotta
PG	=	pale grey	LM	=	lime	PI	=	pink
PO	=	pale orange	PE	=	peach	FU	=	fuchsia
CO	=	coffee	OC	=	ochre	BU	=	burgundy

RS	= right side	FQ = a 22$\frac{1}{2}$in x 20in (57cm x 50cm) piece of fabric,
WS	= wrong side	sold as a Fat quarter

Striped Triangle Quilt

This is a very easy project. Don't get too hung up on making the stripes perfectly rigid. They can wiggle a bit. The fabric behaves best if it is ironed dry when damp. This puts some of the stiffness back and makes it easy to sew the bias edges. Be careful not to tug on the seams as you ease them under the machine presser foot.

SIZE OF QUILT
The finished quilt will measure approximately 90in x 60in (228cm x 152cm).

MATERIALS
Patchwork fabrics:
BS01: 1½yd (1.4m) or 8 FQ
BS06: 1½yd (1.4m) or 8 FQ
NS01: ⅔yd (60cm) or 3 FQ
NS09: ⅔yd (60cm) or 3 FQ
AS01: ¾yd (70cm) or 4 FQ
AS10: 1yd (90cm) or 5 FQ
AS21: ⅔yd (60cm) or 3 FQ
Backing fabric:
NS09: 4¼yd (3.9m)
Binding fabric:
NS09: ¾yd (60cm) or 3 FQ
Batting:
96in x 84in (244cm x 213cm)

PATCH SHAPES
The quilt is made from right-angled triangles, template A. See page 49 for template.

template A

CUTTING OUT
Template A: For 45in- (114cm-) wide fabric, cut 9 strips of fabric 4 1/2 in (11.5cm) wide, with stripes running along the length of the strip. Divide each strip into patches (see page 43). Each FQ will give you 12 patches.
Cut 96 in BS01 and BS06, cut 30 in NS01 and NS09, cut 44 in AS01, 52 in AS10 and cut 36 in AS21.
Bias binding: cut 9yd (8.2m) x 2in (5cm) wide in NS09.
Backing: cut 1 piece 95in x 45in (241cm x 114cm) and 2 pieces 48½in x 22in (123cm x 56cm) in NS09.
Batting: cut 1 piece 96in x 66in (244cm x 168cm).

MAKING THE BLOCKS
There are five different block combinations: for block A use 2 patches of AS01 and AS21; block B use 2 patches of BS01 and BS06; block C use 2 patches

Quilt assembly

Key

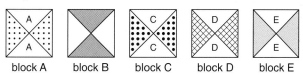

block A   block B   block C   block D   block E

of NS01 and NS09; block D use 2 patches of AS10 and AS21; block E use 2 patches of AS01 and AS10.

Using a ¹⁄₄in (6mm) seam allowance, make up 7-A blocks, 48-B blocks, 15-C blocks, 11-D blocks and 15-E blocks, following the block assembly diagrams.

ASSEMBLING THE BLOCKS

Arrange the 96 blocks into 12 rows of 8 blocks following the quilt assembly

diagram. Join the blocks together into rows, then join the rows together to form the quilt top (see page 44).

Block assembly

FINISHING THE QUILT

Press the assembled quilt top. Seam the 3 backing pieces together with ¹⁄₂in (1.25cm) seam allowance to form 1 piece measuring approximately 96in x 66in (244cm x 168cm). Layer the quilt top, batting, and backing, and baste together (see page 46). Stitch-in-the-ditch diagonally across the centre of each block, but not around the sides, then trim the quilt edges and attach the binding (see page 46).

Striped Triangle Cushion

T his is a very good little project to tackle first, if you are a beginner. Although we haven't quilted the cushion top, this can easily be done, by following the quilting instructions for the Striped Triangle Bag (page 25). You can also make it larger, simply by adding extra blocks.

SIZE OF CUSHION
The finished cushion cover measures approximately 15in x 15in (38cm x 38cm).

MATERIALS
Patchwork, binding and cushion back fabrics:
BS01: $^1/_3$yd (30cm) or 1 FQ
BS06: $^1/_2$yd (45cm) or 1 FQ
NS01: $^1/_2$yd (45cm) or 1 FQ
NS09: $^1/_3$yd (30cm) or 1 FQ
AS10: $^1/_3$yd (30cm) or 1 FQ

AS21: $^1/_8$yd (15cm) or 1 FQ
Cushion pad: 15in x 15in (38cm x 38cm)

PATCH SHAPES
Right-angled triangles, as for Striped Triangle Quilt (see page 22).

CUTTING OUT
Template A: cut 4 in BS01 and BS06, 2 in AS10, AS21, NS01 and NS09, with the grainline arrow following the stripes.

Straight grain binding: cut 2 pieces in NS09 15$^1/_2$in x 3in (39.5cm x 8cm), with the stripes across the width.
Cushion backs: cut 1 large back in BS06 15$^1/_2$in x 11in (39cm x 30cm), with the stripes parallel to the short sides, and cut 1 small back in NS01 15$^1/_2$in x 9$^1/_2$in (39cm x 24cm), with the stripes parallel to the long sides.

MAKING THE BLOCKS
See this section in the Striped Triangle Quilt, and make up 1-C block, 2-B blocks, and 1-D block, following the block assembly diagrams (see page 23).

ASSEMBLING THE BLOCKS
Arrange the 4 blocks into 2 rows of 2 blocks following the cushion assembly diagram. Join the blocks together into rows, then join the rows together to form the cushion top.

Cushion assembly

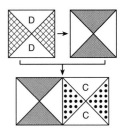

ASSEMBLING THE COVER
Press the assembled cushion top. Bind one long edge of the large and small cushion backs (see page 46).
Lay the cushion top face up on a flat surface and place the small cushion back face down on top, with raw edges level and the bound edge towards the centre. Place the large cushion back face down on top of the uncovered side of the cushion top, keeping raw edges level and overlapping the bound edges by 5in (12.5cm) at the centre.
Baste the cushion cover pieces together around all sides and machine stitch together with a $^3/_8$in (1cm) seam allowance. Turn cover through to right side and insert the cushion pad through the centre back opening.

Striped Triangle Bag

This is the cushion taken a stage further, but it's still easy to do. Many folks avoid stripes because they think they must be lined up so the seams match perfectly. This isn't necessary. In fact they look more exciting if they wiggle a little and don't match just so at the seams. The fun thing about this bag is making the stripes run in so many directions.

SIZE OF BAG
The finished bag measures approximately 15in x 15in (38cm x 38cm).

MATERIALS
Patchwork, strap and gusset, binding and lining fabrics:
BS01: ½yd (45cm) or 1 FQ
BS06: 1¼yd (1m) or 5 FQ
NS01: ½yd (45cm) or 1 FQ
NS09: ½yd (45cm) or 2 FQ
Batting: ¾yd (70cm) x 45in (114cm) wide.

PATCH SHAPES
As for Striped Triangle Quilt (see page 22).

CUTTING OUT
Template A: cut 8 in BS01, BS06, NS01 and NS09, with the grainline arrow following the stripes.
Straight grain binding: cut 7 pieces in BS06 20in x 3in (51cm x 8cm), with the stripes across the width.
Strap and gusset: cut 2 pieces 20in x 2¾in (51cm x 7cm) in both BS06 and NS09 with the stripes across the width of each piece, and 2 pieces in both BS01 and NS01 with the stripes along the length of each piece.
Lining: cut 2 pieces in BS06 18in x 18in (46cm x 46cm).
Batting: cut 2 pieces 18in x 18in (46cm x 46cm) for the bag sides, and 2 pieces 39in x 2¾in (99cm x 7cm) for the strap and gusset.

MAKING THE BLOCKS
See this section in the Striped Triangle Quilt, and make up 4-B blocks, and 4-C blocks following the block assembly diagrams (see page 23).

ASSEMBLING THE BLOCKS
Arrange 4 of the blocks into 2 rows of 2 blocks following the cushion assembly diagram, below. Join the blocks together into 2 rows of 2, then join the rows together to form one bag side. Repeat with the remaining 4 blocks to create the second bag side.

Bag assembly

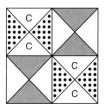

QUILTING THE BAG SIDES
Press the assembled bag sides. Layer the bag sides, batting and linings and baste the pieces together (see page 46). Stitch-in-the-ditch around each block, then stitch 3 square rows of quilting on each block, working the first row ½in (1.25cm) away from the centre of the block and the remaining rows 1 inch (2.5cm) apart. Trim quilt edges and attach a piece of binding to the top edge of each bag side (see page 46).

COMPLETING THE BAG
For full instructions on how to make the strap and gusset and complete the bag, turn to page 47 in the Patchwork Know-how section.

Big Star Quilt

SIZE OF QUILT

The finished quilt will measure approximately 94in x 91in (239cm x 230cm).

MATERIALS

Patchwork fabrics:
Background and binding
GP01-S: 3^1/$_2$yd (3.2m) or 16 FQ
Centre stars
GP09-L: 1^3/$_4$yd (1.5m)
GP09-J: 2yd (1.8m)
GP09-S: 2yd (1.8m)
GP09-C: 2yd (1.8m)
GP09-P: 1^1/$_4$yd (1.2m)
Border half stars
ES04: use remainder from backing
ES20: 1^1/$_4$yd (1.1m) or 5 FQ
Backing fabric:
ES04: 7yd (6.4m)
Batting:
120in x 124in (350cm x 315cm)
Quilting thread:
1 ball of Rowan 4 Ply Cotton

PATCH SHAPES

The patchwork stars for the quilt centre are made from 6 large diamonds (template B).

The half stars at the top and bottom of the quilt centre are made from 2 large diamonds (template B) and 2 large triangles (template D).

The background between the stars is made from the large diamond (template B), the large triangle (template D) and the large equilateral triangle (template C).

10 of the half stars in the border are made from 3 large diamonds (template B), and the remaining 12 from 2 large diamonds (template B), plus 2 large triangles (template D).

The border background is made from the large diamond (template B), the large equilateral triangle (template C) and the large triangle (template D). See pages 49, 50 and 52 for templates.

Templates

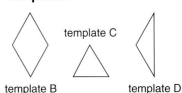

template B   template C   template D

T he fun part of doing this quilt was seeing how the Chards would swirl in unexpected ways. Many of the pieces of Chard were cut from the prettiest parts – the large leaves. Those made nice stars. But it was the pieces cut from the odd ball leftovers which became the best stars when pieced. They were a real surprise. This dramatic quilt was finally enhanced by the use of bold hand quilting.

Quilt assembly

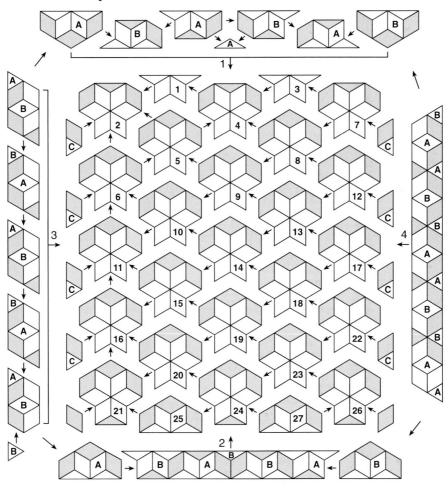

Big star quilt key

centre stars

1	6	15	12	18	24	= GP09-S
2	3	9	20	26		= GP09-P
5	7	16	14	25	23	= GP09-J
4	11	13	22			= GP09-L
8	10	17	19	21	27	= GP09-C

background

☐ = GP01-S

border stars

A = ES20

B = ES04

centre triangles

C = 2 of each GP09-L, GP09-J and GP09-C
1 of each GP09-S, and GP09-P

CUTTING OUT

Centre stars
Template B: fussy cut 4 sets of 6 in GP09-L and P, and 5 sets of 6 in GP09-J, S and C. (see page 43).

Centre half stars
Template B: fussy cut 2 in GP09-J, S, C and P.
Template D: fussy cut 2 in GP09-J, S, C and P.

Centre background
Template B: cut 5$\frac{1}{8}$in- (13cm-) wide strips across the width of the fabric. Each strip will give you 7 patches per 45in- (114cm-) wide fabric, or 3 per FQ (see

page 43). Cut 82 in GP01-S.
Template C: fussy cut 2 in GP09-L, J and C. Cut 1 in GP09-S and P.
Template D: cut 6 in GP01-S.

Border half stars
Template B: cut 5 sets of 3 in ES04 and ES20, and 6 sets of 2 in ES04 and ES20, with the grainline arrow along the stripes. Each FQ will give you 8 patches.
Template C: cut 6 in both ES04 and ES20, with the grainline arrow running along the stripes.
Template D: cut 6 sets of 2, plus 1 extra template in both ES04 and ES20, making sure the grainline arrow is running along

the stripes in all cases.

Border background
Template B: cut 40 in GP01-S, as shown for centre background.
Template C: cut 8 in GP01-S.
Template D: cut 8 in GP01-S.
Straight grain binding: cut 10$\frac{1}{2}$yd x 2$\frac{1}{2}$in (9.6m x 6.5cm) in GP01-S.
Backing: cut 2 pieces 97in x 45in (246cm x 114cm), and 2 pieces 49in x 12in (124cm x 30.5cm) in ES04, with the stripe running along the long sides of each piece.
Batting: cut 1 piece of batting 100in x 97in (254cm x 246cm).

MAKING THE BLOCKS

Using a ¼in (6mm) seam allowance, make up 23 centre stars and 4 half stars for the centre, following the star block assembly diagrams.

Using a ¼in (6mm) seam allowance, make border half stars and corner blocks.

Star block assembly

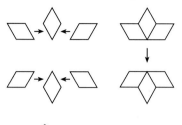

ASSEMBLING THE BLOCKS

Following the quilt assembly diagram in strict order, arrange the centre stars, using the key as a positioning guide. Attach block 1 to block 2, then block 3 to block 4, blocks 4 and 3 to 1, then block 5 to 1, 2 and 4, then block 6 to 2 and 5. Continue in this manner until the centre is complete (see Inset seams page 44).

Following the quilt assembly diagram, arrange border half stars, using key as a positioning guide. Join blocks into 4 rows. Attach the top and bottom borders to the centre, then the side borders, and finally, stitch the corner blocks in place.

FINISHING THE QUILT

Press assembled quilt top. Seam the 4 backing pieces together with ½in (1.25cm) seam allowance to form 1 piece measuring approximately 100in x 97in (254cm x 246cm). Layer quilt top, batting, and backing. Baste together (see page 46). To hand quilt the stars and half stars, work a row of stitches to join the very pointed ends of each diamond (see page 46). Work a second row of stitches to join the two shallow points, forming a cross in the centre of each diamond. For the background work a row of stitches to join only the very pointed ends of each diamond, and for each triangle a row that bisects it in half at 90 degrees.

Trim the quilt edges and attach the binding (see page 46).

Baby Star Quilt

This quilt is offered in two colourways, one pastel and the other in rich jewel tones, creating two totally different looks - choose which one you prefer. To produce the soft subtle shades and tones of this quilt a lot of the centre stars are made using the wrong side of the fabric as the right side. To finish, the quilt layers are then gently tied together with a creamy coloured Botany wool.

Quilt assembly

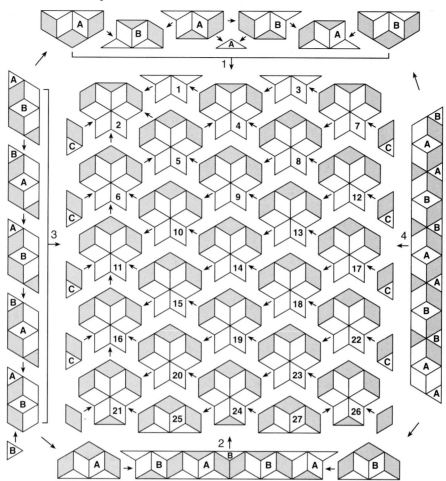

Baby star quilt key

centre stars

1	13	24	= GP06-C
2	14		= GP01-P
6	18		= GP03-P
5	22		= GP09-P
4	25	26	= GP01-S(W.S.)
3	20		= GP03-S

7	21	= GP09-C
8	16	= GP01-C
9	27	= GP03-L(W.S.)
10		= GP06-J(W.S.)
11	19	12	= GP01-L(W.S.)
15	23	= GP04-C(W.S.)
17		= GP06-S

background

☐ = GP06-P

border stars

A B = GP06-L

centre triangles

C = random colours from centre stars

SIZE OF QUILT

The finished quilt will measure approximately 42in x 40in (106cm x 101cm).

MATERIALS

Patchwork fabrics:
Background
GP06-P: 1yd (90cm) or 3 FQ
Centre stars
GP06-J: ⅛yd (11cm) or 1 FQ

GP06-S: ⅛yd (11cm) or 1 FQ
GP06-C: ¼yd (23cm) or 1 FQ
GP01-L: ¼yd (23cm) or 1 FQ
GP01-S: ¼yd (23cm) or 1 FQ
GP01-C: ¼yd (23cm) or 1 FQ
GP01-P: ¼yd (23cm) or 1 FQ
GP03-L: ½yd (45cm) or 1 FQ
GP03-S: ½yd (45cm) or 1 FQ
GP03-P: ½yd (45cm) or 1 FQ
GP09-C: ½yd (45cm) or 1 FQ
GP09-P: ½yd (45cm) or 1 FQ

GP04-C: ¼yd (23cm) or 1 FQ
Border half stars
GP06-L: ¾yd (70cm) or 2 FQ
Backing fabric:
GP06-J: 1½yd (1.4m)
Binding fabric:
GP01-P: ½yd (45cm) or 1 FQ
Batting:
60in x 45in (152cm x 114cm)
Tying yarn:
1 ball of Rowan True 4 Ply Botany yarn

29

PATCH SHAPES

The patchwork stars for the quilt centre are made from 6 small diamonds (template E).

The half stars at the top and bottom of the quilt centre are made from 2 small diamonds (template E) and 2 small triangles (template G).

The background between the stars is made from the small diamond (template E), the small triangle (template G) and the small equilateral triangle (template F). 10 of the half stars in the border are made from 3 small diamonds (template E), and the remaining 12 from 2 small diamonds (template E), plus 2 small triangles (template G).

The border background is made from the small diamond (template E), the small equilateral triangle (template F) and the small triangle (template G). See page 49 for templates.

Templates

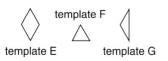

template F

template E   template G

CUTTING OUT

Centre stars

Template E: cut 2$\frac{1}{2}$in- (6.5cm-) wide strips of fabric. Each strip should give you 14 patches per 45in- (114cm-) wide fabric, or 7 patches per FQ (see page 43). Cut 1 set of 6 in GP06-J (WS) and S, 2 sets of 6 in GP06-C, GP01-S (WS), C, P and GP04-C (WS), 3 sets of 6 in GP01-L (WS).

Fussy cut (see page 43) 1 set of 6 in GP03-L (WS) and S, 2 sets of 6 in GP03-P, GP09-C and P.

Centre half stars

Template E: fussy cut 2 in GP03-L (WS), S, GP06-C and GP01-S (WS).
Template G: fussy cut 2 in GP03-L (WS), S, GP06-C and GP01-S (WS).

Centre background

Template E: cut 2$\frac{1}{2}$in- (6.5cm-) wide strips across the width of the fabric. Each strip will give you 14 patches per 45in- (114cm-) wide fabric, or 7 patches per FQ (see page 43). Cut 82 in GP06-P.
Template F: cut 8 in random fabrics from centre stars.
Template G: cut 6 in GP06-P.

Border half stars

Template E: cut 10 sets of 3 and 12 sets of 2 in GP06-L, as shown for the centre background.

Template F: cut 12 in GP06-L.
Template G: cut 26 in GP06-L.

Border background

Template E: cut 40 in GP06-P, as shown for centre background.
Template F: cut 8 in GP06-P.
Template G: cut 8 in GP06-P.

Straight grain binding: cut 4$\frac{3}{4}$yd x 1$\frac{3}{4}$in (4.3m x 4.5cm) in GP01-P.

Backing: cut 1 piece 47in x 45in (120cm x 114cm) in GP06-J.

Batting: cut 1 piece 47in x 45in (120cm x 114cm).

MAKING THE BLOCKS

Using a $\frac{1}{4}$in (6mm) seam allowance, make up 23 centre stars and 4 half stars for the centre, following the star block assembly diagrams.

Using a $\frac{1}{4}$in (6mm) seam allowance, make border half stars and corner blocks.

Star block assembly

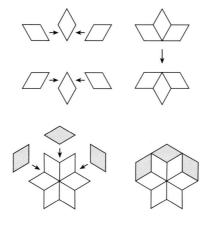

ASSEMBLING THE BLOCKS

Following the quilt assembly diagram in strict order, arrange the centre stars, using the key as a positioning guide. Attach block 1 to block 2, then block 3 to block 4; blocks 4 and 3 to 1, then block 5 to 1, 2 and 4, then block 6 to 2 and 5; block 7 to 3; block 8 to 7, 3 and 4; block 9 to 4, 5 and 8; block 10 to 5, 6 and 9; and block 11 to 6 and 10. Continue in this manner until the centre is complete (see page 44). Following the quilt assembly diagram, arrange border half stars, using key as a positioning guide. Join blocks into 4 rows. Attach the top and bottom borders to the centre, then the side borders, and finally, stitch the corner blocks in place.

FINISHING THE QUILT

Press the assembled quilt top. Layer the quilt top, batting, and backing, and baste together (see page 46). Make ties at each of the star points to hold the quilt layers together. Using a darning needle and a length of yarn, stitch through all layers where the tie will be. Make a second stitch at the same place (Fig A), and knot ends together on the right side of the quilt (Fig B). Then, make a second knot to secure (Fig C). After working all the ties, trim the ends to the desired length. Trim the quilt edges and attach the binding (see page 46).

Figure A

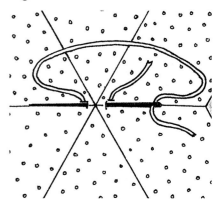

Figure B

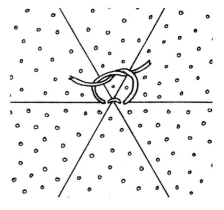

Figure C

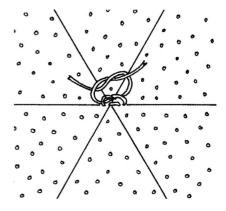

Dark Star Quilt

By using rich jewel tones, a stunningly different look is created with this design, from the Baby Star Quilt. Some of the stripes used are cut very carefully and arranged so they swirl. A few are cut any which way. These cockeyed ones add to the interest in this design. They make it less predictable and hold your attention.

SIZE OF QUILT
The finished quilt will measure approximately 42in x 40in (106cm x 101cm).

MATERIALS
Patchwork fabrics:
Background
GP01-J: 1yd (90cm) or 3 FQ

Centre stars
NS17: ¹⁄₃yd (30cm) or 1 FQ
AS10: ¹⁄₂yd (45cm) or 1 FQ
BS01: ¹⁄₃yd (30cm) or 1 FQ
PS01: ¹⁄₂yd (45cm) or 1 FQ
PS13: ¹⁄₂yd (45cm) or 1 FQ
ES10: ¹⁄₃yd (30cm) or 1 FQ
ES15: ¹⁄₃yd (30cm) or 1 FQ
ES23: ¹⁄₄yd (23cm) or 1 FQ
GP09-J: 1¹⁄₄yd (1.1m) or 2 FQ
GP03-J: ¹⁄₂yd (45cm) or 1 FQ

Border half stars
NS09: ²⁄₃yd (60cm) or 2 FQ
NS17: ²⁄₃yd (60cm) or 2 FQ

Backing fabric:
GP03-J: 1¹⁄₂yd (1.4m)

Binding fabric:
PS15: ¹⁄₂yd (45cm) or 2 FQ

Batting:
60in x 45in (152cm x 114cm)

PATCH SHAPES
The patchwork stars for the quilt centre are made from 6 small diamonds (template E).
The half stars at the top and bottom of the quilt centre are made from 2 small diamonds (template E) and 2 small triangles (template G).
The background between the stars is made from the small diamond (template E), the small triangle (template G) and the small equilateral triangle (template F).
10 of the half stars in the border are made from 3 small diamonds (template E), and the remaining 12 from 2 small diamonds (template E), plus 2 small triangles (template G).
The border background is made from the small diamond (template E), the small equilateral triangle (template F) and the small triangle (template G). See page 49

Quilt assembly

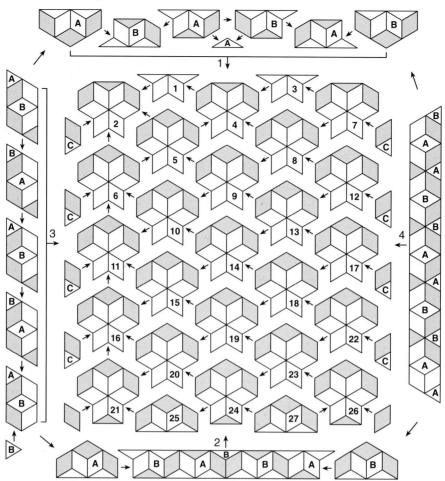

Dark star quilt key

centre stars

1	10	12				= NS17
2	21	23				= AS10
6	26					= BS01
5	7	11	18	24	27	= GP09-J
4	17					= PS01
3	9	20				= GP03-J

8	14	25	= ES10
16	19		= ES15
15	22		= PS13
13			= ES23

background

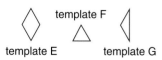	= GP01-J

border stars

A	= NS17
B	= NSO9

centre triangles

C	= 2 of each AS10, PSO1, PS13 and ES23

Templates

template E template F template G

CUTTING OUT

Centre stars

Template E: placing each set on different grains to produce a kaleidoscopic effect, cut 1 set of 6 ES23.

Cut 2 sets of 6 in ES15, NS17, BS01, PS01, PS13, ES10 and GP03-J.

Cut 3 sets of 6 in AS10.

Cut 5 sets in GP09-J.

Centre half stars

Template E: fussy cut 2 sets in GP09-J, GP03-J, NS17 and ES10.

Template G: fussy cut 2 sets in GP09-J, GP03-J, NS17 and ES10.

Centre background

Template E: cut 2½in- (6.5cm-) wide strips across the width of the fabric. Each strip will give you 14 patches per 45in- (114cm-) wide fabric, or 7 per FQ (see page 43). Cut 82 in GP01-J.

Template F: cut 2 of each in AS10, PS01, PS13 and ES23, cutting half with the stripes right up the centre and half with stripes along one edge.

Template G: cut 6 in GP01-J.

Border half stars

Template E: cut 5 sets of 3 in NS09 and NS17, and 6 sets of 2 in NS09 and NS17, placing the grainline arrow so stripes run right up the centre of each diamond.

Template F: cut 6 in NS09 and NS17,

placing the grainline arrow so stripes run right up the centre of each triangle.

Template G: cut 6 sets of 2, plus 1 extra in both NS09 and NS17, with the grainline arrow along the stripes.

Border background

Template E: cut 40 in GP01-J, as shown for centre background.

Template F: cut 8 in GP01-J.

Template G: cut 8 in GP01-J.

Bias binding: cut 4³/₄yd x 1³/₄in (4.3m x 4.5cm) in PS15.

Backing: cut 1 piece 47in x 45in (120cm x 114cm) in GP03-J.

Batting: cut 1 piece 47in x 45in (120cm x 114cm).

MAKING THE BLOCKS

See this section in the Baby Star Quilt (page 30).

ASSEMBLING THE BLOCKS

Following the quilt assembly diagram in strict order, arrange the centre stars, using the key as a positioning guide. Attach block 1 to 2, then 3 to 4, then 4 and 3 to 1. Continue in this manner until the centre is complete (see page 44).

Following the quilt assembly diagram, arrange border half stars, using key as a positioning guide. Join blocks into 4 rows. Attach the top and bottom borders to the centre, then the side borders, and finally, stitch the corner blocks in place.

FINISHING THE QUILT

Press the assembled quilt top. Layer the quilt top, batting, and backing, and baste together (see page 46). Spiral stitch over the entire quilt using an eggplant coloured thread. Start at the centre and work out to the sides in an uneven hexagonal shape spaced roughly 1in (2.5cm) apart (see quilting diagram). Trim quilt edges and attach the binding (see page 46).

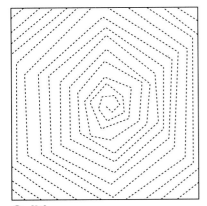

Quilting

Jewel and Stone Star Cushions ★★

This is an exciting project, where you can really go to town on the quilting. We machine quilted, working from the centre of the stars and radiating stitchlines out along the leaf stalks on each diamond, free-quilting the remaining patches in a 'bubbly' fashion. This would also be a fun project to hand quilt, with bold stitches, like the Big Star Quilt.

SIZE OF CUSHION

The finished cushion cover measures 18in x 16in (46cm x 41cm).

MATERIALS

Jewel patchwork, binding and cushion back fabrics:
GP01-J: ²/₃yd (60cm) or 3 FQ
GP09-J: ¹/₃yd (30cm)

Stone patchwork, binding and cushion back fabrics:
GP01-S: ²/₃yd (60cm) or 3 FQ
GP09-S: ¹/₃yd (30cm)

Backing fabric: 1yd (90cm) x 45in- (114cm-) wide lining.

Batting: 1yd (90cm) x 45in (114cm) wide.

Cushion pad: 18in x18in (45cm x 45cm).

PATCH SHAPES

The centre star is made from 6 large diamonds (template B). The background is made from 2 large triangles (template D) and 4 corner blocks (template H). See pages 50, 51 and 52 for templates.

Templates

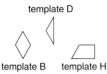

template D

template B   template H

CUTTING OUT

Template B: fussy cut 1 set of 6 in GP09-J or S, placing 3 of each on the alternate leaf colours.

Template D: cut 2 in GP01-J or S.

Template H: cut 2(RS) and 2(WS) in GP01-J or S.

Straight grain binding: cut 2 pieces in GP09-J or S 18in x 3in (46cm x 8cm).

Cushion backs: cut 1 large back in GP01-J or S 16½in x 13in (42cm x 33cm). Cut 1 small back in GP01-J or S 16½in x 10½in (42cm x 27cm).

Backing: cut 1 front piece 20½in x 18½in (52cm x 46cm). Cut 1 large back in GP01-J or S 18½in x 15in (52cm x 38cm). Cut 1 small back in GP01-J or S 18½in x 12½in (52cm x 32cm).

Batting: cut 1 front and 2 backs to measurements given for the backing.

ASSEMBLING QUILT TOP

Using a ¼in (6mm) seam allowance, make up centre star, alternating diamond colours and following Star block assembly diagram in the Big Star Quilt, page 28. Attach top and bottom triangles and corner blocks, following Cushion and Bag assembly diagram.

Cushion and bag assembly

Jewel star key

☐ = GP09-J

▨ = GP01-J

Stone star key

☐ = GP09-S

▨ = GP01-S

QUILTING THE TOP

Press assembled cushion top. Layer quilt top, batting, backing and baste together. Stitch-in-the-ditch around each patch, then free-motion quilt the individual patch shapes, using quilting diagrams as a guide (see opposite). Trim quilt edges.

FINISHING OFF THE COVER

Layer large cushion back, batting, backing and baste together. Repeat with small back. Work straight rows of quilting parallel to long sides, spaced 2in (5cm) apart. Trim quilt edges. To assemble the cover, see this section in the Striped Triangle Cushion (page 24).

Jewel and Stone Star Bag ★★

When making the Big Star Quilt, several more Chard stars were made than were needed. This gave more choices when assembling the quilt. This very useful bag was another great way to use up the extra stars.

SIZE OF BAG

The finished bag measures approximately 18in x 16in (46cm x 41cm).

MATERIALS

Jewel patchwork, strap and gusset, binding and lining fabrics:
GP01-J: 1⅔yd (1.5m)
GP09-J: ⅔yd (60cm)

Stone patchwork, strap and gusset, binding and lining fabrics:
GP01-S: 1⅔yd (1.5m)
GP09-S: ⅔yd (60cm)

Batting: ¾yd (70cm) x 45in (114cm) wide.

PATCH SHAPES

The centre star is made from 6 large diamonds (template B). The background is made from 2 large triangles (template D) and 4 corner blocks (template H). See pages 50, 51 and 52 for templates.

Templates

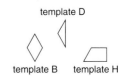

template D

template B   template H

CUTTING OUT

Template B: fussy cut 2 sets of 6 in GP09-J or S, placing 6 of each on the alternate leaf colours.

Template D: cut 4 in GP01-J or S.

Template H: cut 4(RS) and 4(WS) in GP01-J or S.

Straight grain binding: cut 4 pieces in GP01-J or S 45in x 3in (114cm x 8cm).

Strap and gusset: cut 4 pieces 41^3/4in x 2^3/4in (106cm x 7cm) GP01-J or S.

Lining: cut 2 pieces in GP01-J or S, 20^1/2in x 18^1/2in (52cm x 47cm).

Batting: cut 2 pieces 20^1/2in x 18^1/2in (52cm x 47cm) for the bag sides, and 2 pieces 41^1/2in x 2^3/4in (105cm x 7cm) for the strap and gusset.

ASSEMBLING QUILT TOP

Using a ^{1}/4in (6mm) seam allowance, make up centre star, alternating diamond colours and following Star block assembly diagram in the Big Star Quilt, page 28. Attach top and bottom triangles and corner blocks, following Cushion and Bag assembly diagram.

Cushion and bag assembly

Jewel star key

☐ = GP09-J

▨ = GP01-J

Stone star key

☐ = GP09-S

▨ = GP01-S

QUILTING THE BAG SIDES

To make one bag side, press assembled quilt top. Layer quilt top, batting, backing and baste together. Stitch-in-the-ditch around each patch, then free-motion quilt the individual patch shapes, using quilting diagrams as a guide. Trim quilt edges. Attach a piece of binding to the top edge (see page 46). Repeat for second bag side.

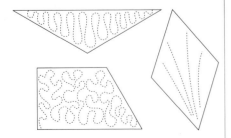

COMPLETING THE BAG

For instructions on how to complete the bag, turn to page 47 in the Patchwork Know-how section, but remember you only have 4 pieces to each strap and gusset, NOT 8.

Magenta Floating Blocks Quilt ★★

We chose to ignore the grainlines when cutting the patches for this quilt, to create a kaleidoscopic effect. For your ease we have grouped the stripes into three shade groups, but feel free to do your own grouping and crossover of colours, to develop other interesting effects.

Quilt assembly

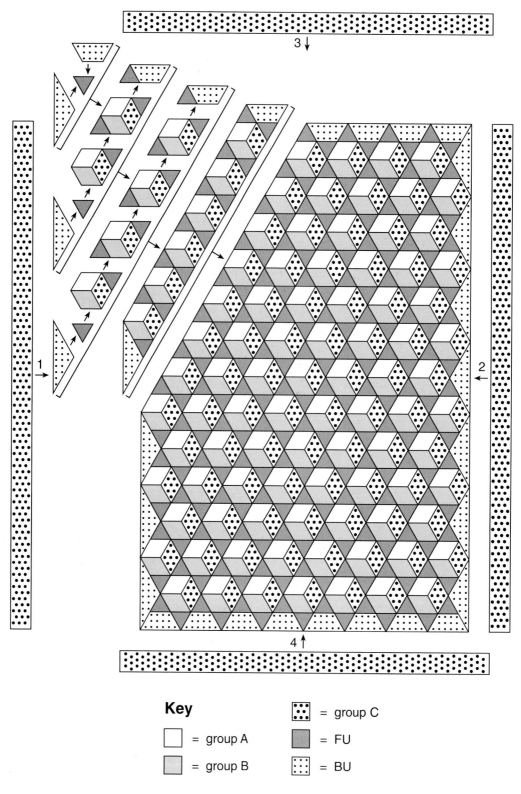

Key

☐ = group A

▨ = group B

▦ = group C

▦ = FU

⊡ = BU

SIZE OF QUILT

The finished quilt will measure approximately 80in x 55in (203cm x 140cm).

MATERIALS

Patchwork fabrics:

Group A – light shades

NS16: ¹/₄yd (25cm) or 1 FQ

PS04: ¹/₄yd (25cm) or 1 FQ
ES04: see backing fabric
BS11: ¹/₄yd (25cm) or 1 FQ
BS23: ¹/₄yd (25cm) or 1 FQ

Group B – medium shades

AS10: ¹/₄yd (25cm) or 1 FQ
NS01: ¹/₄yd (25cm) or 1 FQ
ES10: ¹/₄yd (25cm) or 1 FQ
BS01: ¹/₄yd (25cm) or 1 FQ

BS06: ¹/₄yd (25cm) or 1 FQ

Group C – dark shades

ES01: ¹/₄yd (25cm) or 1 FQ
ES21: see border fabric
NS09: ¹/₄yd (25cm) or 1 FQ
NS17: ¹/₄yd (25cm) or 1 FQ
PS08: ¹/₄yd (25cm) or 1 FQ

Plain background fabrics

FU: 1¹/₈yd (1m) x 45in (114cm) wide

BU: $^2/_3$yd (60cm) x 45in (114cm) wide
Border fabric:
ES21: $^2/_3$yd (60cm) or 2 FQ
Backing fabric:
ES04: $3^2/_3$yd (3.4m)
Binding fabric:
NS17: $^2/_3$yd (60cm) or 2 FQ
Batting:
96in x 60in (244cm x 152cm)

PATCH SHAPES
The quilt centre is made from blocks of 3 small diamonds (template J). The background between the blocks is made from a single equilateral triangle (template L), and the edges of the quilt centre are made from one large triangle (template K) and a trapezoid shape (template M). See pages 50, 51 and 53 for the templates.

Templates

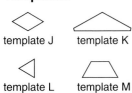

template J   template K

template L   template M

CUTTING OUT
Centre blocks group A:
Template J: cut on varying grainlines 19 in NS16, PS04 and BS23. Cut 20 in ES04 and BS11.
Centre blocks group B:
Template J: cut on varying grainlines 19 in ES10, BS01 and BS06. Cut 20 in AS10 and NS01.

Centre blocks group C:
Template J: cut on varying grainlines 19 in ES01, ES21 and NS17. Cut 20 in NS09 and PS08.

Background:
Template L: cut $3^1/_2$in- (9cm-) wide strips across the width of the fabric. Each strip will give you 21 patches (see page 43). Cut 210 in FU.
Template K: cut $3^1/_2$in- (9cm-) wide strips across the width of the fabric. Each strip gives you 5 patches. Cut 14 in BU.
Template M: cut $3^1/_8$in- (8cm-) wide strips across width of fabric. Each strip will give you 8 patches. Cut 16 in BU.

Borders:
Cut 8 side strips and 6 end strips 20in x $3^3/_4$in (50cm x 9.5cm) wide, with stripes across width in ES21.
Straight grain binding: cut $7^2/_3$yd x $2^1/_2$in (7m x 6.5cm) in NS17 with stripes across width.

Backing: cut 2 pieces 61in x $43^1/_2$in (155cm x 110cm) in ES04.
Batting: cut 1 piece 86in x 61in (218cm x 155cm).

MAKING THE BLOCKS
Select 1 diamond from each of the fabric groups A, B and C. Arrange the 3 patches following the block assembly diagram, right. Using a $^1/_4$in (6mm) seam allowance, stitch the bottom patches together, then the top diamond, using an inset seam (see page 44). Stitch a small background triangle (template L) to each side of the block.

Make a total of 85 blocks, positioning the light, medium and dark fabrics consistently throughout to give the quilt an illusion that a 'light source' is coming from one direction.
For the left hand side of the quilt, make 6 blocks with only 1 background triangle attached to the dark coloured diamond, and for the right hand side, make 6 blocks with 1 background triangle attached to the medium coloured diamond.

ASSEMBLING THE BLOCKS
Following the quilt assembly diagram in strict order, arrange the centre of the quilt in diagonal rows. The first row is made from a large (K template) triangle, a small (L template) background triangle and a trapezoid (template M).
The second row is made from a large (K template) triangle, a small (L template) background triangle, a left hand diamond block, a full diamond block and a small (L template) background triangle attached to a trapezoid (template M).
Row 3 is the same as 2, but with 3 full diamond blocks. Continue in this manner until the quilt is laid out in diagonal rows. Using a $^1/_4$in (6mm) seam allowance, join the blocks together into rows, then join

the rows together to form the quilt top (see page 44).
Join the side border strips to form 2 strips $73^1/_2$in (187cm) long and the end borders to form 2 strips 55in (140cm) long. Attach the 2 side borders to the edges of the quilt and then the end borders.

Diamond block assembly

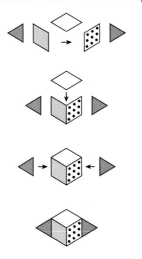

FINISHING THE QUILT
Press the assembled quilt top. Seam the 2 backing pieces together with $^1/_2$in (1.25cm) seam allowance to form 1 piece measuring approximately 86in x 61in (218cm x 155cm). Layer the quilt top, batting, and backing, and baste together (see page 46). Stitch-in-the-ditch around each patch, then free-motion quilt all the plain background patches, using the quilting diagrams as a guide.
Trim the quilt edges and attach the binding (see page 46).

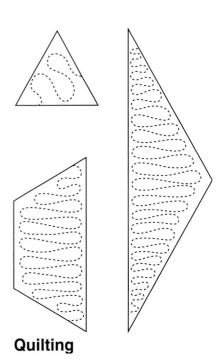

Quilting

Ochre Pennants Tablecloth

This project appears to be very difficult. All those sharp pointy bits! But even a novice patchworker could do this project. The secret is to use foundation papers. By sewing through paper patterns following the straight lines, the patchwork becomes really easy to do!

SIZE OF THE CLOTH

The finished cloth measures approximately 66$\frac{1}{2}$in x 66$\frac{1}{2}$in (169cm x 169cm).

MATERIALS

Striped patchwork fabrics:
AS21: see backing fabric
PS04: $\frac{1}{2}$yd (45cm) or 2 FQ
PS08: $\frac{1}{2}$yd (45cm) or 2 FQ
PS14: $\frac{2}{3}$yd (60cm) or 2 FQ
ES10: $\frac{2}{3}$yd (60cm) or 2 FQ
ES20: 1yd (90cm) or 2 FQ
ES23: $\frac{1}{3}$yd (30cm) or 1 FQ
NS01: 1yd (90cm) or 2 FQ
NS16: $\frac{2}{3}$yd (60cm) or 2 FQ
BS01: $\frac{2}{3}$yd (60cm) or 1 FQ
BS11: $\frac{1}{2}$yd (45cm) or 2 FQ
Plain patchwork fabrics:
OC: 1$\frac{2}{3}$yd (1.5m) x 45in (114cm) wide
TE: 1yd (90cm) x 45in (114cm) wide
PI: 1$\frac{1}{2}$yd (1.4m) x 45in (114cm) wide
Backing and binding fabric:
AS21: 4$\frac{1}{2}$yd (4.1m)

PATCH SHAPES

The tablecloth centre is made from 2 blocks of triangles that are exactly the same size. The blocks are made up using the foundation-piecing method. The finished blocks R and S measure 6in x 6in (15cm x15cm).
The border is made from 2 triangles, a large isosceles triangle (template N) and 2 small right-angled triangles (template P and template P-reversed). See pages 51 and 52 for the templates.

Templates and foundation blocks

template N   template P

R   S

Tablecloth assembly

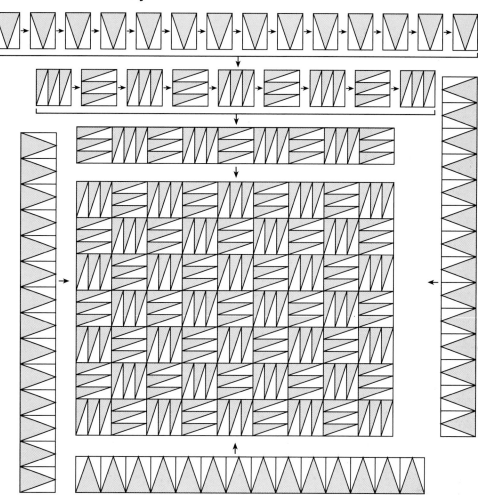

Key

☐ = striped fabrics

▨ = plain fabrics

FOUNDATION PAPERS

The foundation papers used for this patchwork are given on pages 53 and 54. Make 41 copies of block R and 40 copies of block S. Note, the R-reverse foundation block is used for the 'vertical' squares in the patchwork.

CUTTING OUT

Border:

Template N: cut strips of fabric 7in (18cm) wide. Each strip will give 16 patches per 45in- (114cm-) wide fabric (see page 43). Cut 21 in OC, 15 in TE and 20 in PI.

Template P: cut strips of fabric 7¾in

(19.5cm) wide. Each strip will give you 25 patches per 45in- (114cm-) wide fabric, or 12 per FQ. Cut 4 in ES23, 5 in PS14, 6 in ES10 and PS08, 7 in ES20 and NS16, 10 in NS01 and 12 in BS01 with the stripes along the long edge.

Template P-reversed: cut strips of fabric 2¾in (7cm) wide. Each strip will give you 10 patches per 45in- (114cm-) wide fabric, or 4 per FQ. Cut 4 in ES23 and PS14, 5 in ES10, 6 in PS08, 7 in ES20, 8 in NS16, 10 in NS01 and 11 in BS01 with stripes along the short edge.

Backing: cut 1 piece 66½in x 45in (169cm x 114cm) and cut 1 piece 66½in x 22½in (169 x 57cm) in AS21.

Straight grain binding: cut 7½yd x 2½in (6.9m x 6.5cm) in AS21 with stripes across width.

Centre pieces:

Cut the remaining stripe and plain fabrics into 3-4in- (7.7-8cm-) wide strips of any length. Cut strips into 8in (20cm) lengths and then cut them diagonally from one corner to the other. You will need at least 51 in TE, 86 in PI, 105 in OC, 9 in NS16, 11 in ES23 and PS08, 15 in BS01, 19 in ES10, 26 in NS01, 28 in BS11, 29 in PS04, 31 in AS21 and 33in ES20.

Note: The paper foundation will give your blocks stability. This means that you can ignore the grainline on the fabrics and cut the patches at varying angles to create a more lively effect. This also means you can use up all your scraps!

MAKING THE CENTRE BLOCKS

Make the blocks using the foundation papers and following the instructions for foundation-piecing on page 45. Use plain fabrics for the even-numbered areas and stripes for the odd-numbered areas. Pick up patches at random, or arrange them first to get an overall effect. Make up 41 R-blocks and 40 S-blocks.

MAKING THE BORDER BLOCKS

Using a $1/4$in (6mm) seam allowance, make 56 border blocks, by joining a P template triangle and a P-reversed triangle to an N template triangle, as shown in the block assembly diagram.

Border block assembly

ASSEMBLING THE CENTRE BLOCKS

Arrange the patches in 9 rows of 9 blocks, alternating the R and S blocks, as shown in the assembly diagram. Using a $1/4$in (6mm) seam allowance, join the blocks together into rows, then join the rows together to form the tablecloth centre (see page 44).

ASSEMBLING THE BORDER BLOCKS

Arrange the border blocks into 4 rows of 14 blocks. Using a $1/4$in (6mm) seam allowance, join the blocks together into the 4 border strips following the tablecloth assembly diagram. Attach the borders, butting the ends together at each corner.

FINISHING TABLECLOTH

Press the assembled tablecloth top. Seam the 2 backing pieces together with $1/2$in (1.25cm) seam allowance to form 1 piece measuring approximately $66^{1}/2$in x $66^{1}/2$in (169cm x 169cm). Layer the cloth top and backing, and baste together (see page 46). Attach the binding to the edges (see page 46).

Pastel Tumbling Blocks Quilt ★★★

Although this quilt is machine pieced, it lends itself perfectly to being made up by hand using the 'English paper piecing' technique – in which case, it becomes a great 'traveling' project, that can go with you on vacations or even business trips!

SIZE OF QUILT

The finished quilt will measure approximately 94in x 67¹/₂in (240cm x 172cm).

MATERIALS

Print patchwork fabrics:
GP06-J: ²/₃yd (60cm) or 2 FQ
GP06-S: ²/₃yd (60cm) or 2 FQ
GP06-C: ¹/₂yd (45cm) or 2 FQ
GP06-P: ¹/₂yd (45cm) or 2 FQ
GP04-L: ¹/₃yd (30cm) or 1 FQ
GP04-C: ¹/₂yd (45cm) or 2 FQ
GP04-P: ¹/₄yd (25cm) or 1 FQ
GP03-S: ¹/₂yd (45cm) or 2 FQ
GP03-P: ¹/₂yd (45cm) or 2 FQ
GP09-C: ¹/₄yd (25cm) or 1 FQ
GP09-P: ²/₃yd (60cm) or 2 FQ
GP01-P: ¹/₄yd (25cm) or 1 FQ

Plain patchwork fabrics:
PE: ¹/₂yd (45cm) x 45in (114cm) wide
LC: ¹/₂yd (45cm) x 45in (114cm) wide
LM: ²/₃yd (60cm) x 45in (114cm) wide
PO: ²/₃yd (60cm) x 45in (114cm) wide
PG: see outer border fabric
PBL: ¹/₂yd (45cm) x 45in (114cm) wide
CO: 1yd (90cm) x 45in (114cm) wide

Backing and binding fabric:
GP04-C: 5¹/₂yd (5m)

Print inner border fabric:
GP06-J: 1yd (90cm) or 3 FQ

Plain outer border fabric:
PG: ²/₃yd (60cm) x 45in (114cm) wide

Batting:
120in x 124in (305cm x 315cm)

PATCH SHAPES

The quilt centre is made from blocks of 3 small diamonds (template J).
The half blocks, on alternate rows down the sides, are made from 1 small diamond (template J) and 1 small equilateral triangle (template L). The top and bottom edges of the central patchwork are filled

with a large triangle (template Q) and a small right-angled triangle (template T and T-reversed) at the corners. See pages 49, 50 and 51 for templates.

CUTTING OUT

Centre blocks
Template J: cut 3¹/₄in- (8.5cm-) wide strips across the width of the fabric. Each strip will give you 11 patches for 45in- (114cm-) wide fabric and 5 per FQ (see page 44).
Cut 12 in GP04-P, GP09-C, GP06-J(WS) and GP01-P, 24 in GP04-L(WS), 33 in GP06-C, 34 in GP03-S, 36 in GP06-P, GP03-P, GP04-C, GP06-J(RS), PE, LC and PBL, 47 in GP06-S, GP09-P, LM and CO and 48 in PO and PG.
Template L: cut 2 in GP09-P, GP06-S, LM, CO, 4 in GP03-S, 6 in GP06-C.
Template Q: cut 2in- (5cm-) wide strips across the width of fabric. Each strip will give you 11 patches. Cut 22 in CO.
Template T: cut 2 in CO.
Template T-reversed: cut 2 in CO.

Inner borders:
Cut 6 side strips in GP04-J, 32in x 2¹/₂in (81cm x 6.5cm), using 45in- (114cm-) wide fabric, or 10 strips 22in x 2¹/₂in (57cm x 6.5cm) for a FQ.
Cut 4 end strips in GP04-J, 32in x 2¹/₂in (81cm x 6.5cm), using 45cm-wide fabric, or 6 strips 22in x 2¹/₂in (57cm x 6.5cm) for a FQ.

Outer borders:
Cut 6 side strips 33in x 1³/₄in (84cm x 4.5cm) wide, and 4 end strips 34in x 1³/₄in (86cm x 4.5cm) in PG.

Straight grain binding: cut 9¹/₈yd x 2¹/₂in (8.3m x 6.5cm) in GP04-C.

Backing: cut 2 pieces 73in x 45in (185cm x 114cm) and 2 pieces 37in x 12in (94cm x 30cm) in GP04-C.

Batting: cut 1 piece 100in x 73in (254cm x 185cm).

MAKING THE BLOCKS

Arrange 3 diamonds following the block assembly diagram. Using ¹/₄in (6mm) seam allowance, stitch the bottom patches together, then the top diamond using an inset seam (see page 44).
Make a total of 120 blocks and 18 half-blocks, following the key and making sure you position the fabrics in the right place each time.

Block assembly

ASSEMBLING THE BLOCKS

Following the key and quilt assembly diagram in strict order (see overleaf), arrange the 12 blocks for the top row of the patchwork centre. Next, arrange 11 blocks and 2 half-blocks for the second row. Continue in this manner until the whole of the centre is laid out.
Using a ¹/₄in (6mm) seam allowance, join the blocks together into the rows, then join the rows together, using inset seams. Stitch the large triangles to the top and bottom edges, with inset seams, and attach the corner triangles.

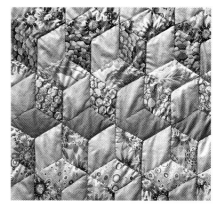

MAKING THE BORDERS

Join the inner side border strips to form 2 strips 91¹/₂in (232cm) long and the inner end borders to form 2 strips 63¹/₂in (161cm) long. Attach the 2 end borders to the edges of the quilt and then the side borders. Repeat in the same order with the outer borders, forming 2 side strips 94in (231cm) long and 2 ends 67¹/₂in (171cm) long.

FINISHING THE QUILT

Press the assembled quilt top. Seam the 3 backing pieces together with ¹/₂in (1.25cm) seam allowance to form 1 piece measuring approximately 100in x 73in (254cm x 185cm). Layer the quilt top, batting and backing, and baste together (see page 46). Stitch-in-the-ditch around each block and the borders.
Trim the quilt edges and attach the binding (see page 46).

Templates

template J

template L

template Q

template T

Quilt assembly

Key

centre blocks

= fabric positions

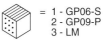
= 1 - GP03-P
2 - GP06-S
3 - PE

= 1 - LM
2 - GP09-C
3 - PG

= 1 - GP06-S
2 - GP04-C
3 - PBL

= 1 - GP03-S
2 - GP06-J(R.S.)
3 - LC

= 1 - GP09-P
2 - GP04-L(W.S.)
3 - LM

= 1 - CO
2 - GP03-P
3 - PO

= 1 - GP01-P
2 - GP03-S
3 - PG

= 1 - GP09-P
2 - GP06-J(R.S.)
3 - PE

= 1 - GP06-P
2 - GP04-L(W.S.)
3 - PG

= 1 - GP06-C
2 - CO
3 - PO

= 1 - GP06-J(R.S.)
2 - GP06-P
3 - PE

= 1 - GP06-S
2 - GP09-P
3 - LM

= 1 - GP04-P
2 - GP03-P
3 - LC

= 1 - GP06-C
2 - GP04-C
3 - PBL

= 1 - GP06-S
2 - CO
3 - PO

= 1 - GP03-S
2 - GP06-J(WS.)
3 - LC

= 1 - GP09-P
2 - GP04-C
3 - LM

= 1 - GP06-C
2 - CO
3 - PO

= 1 - PG
2 - GP06-P
3 - PBL

borders

= GP04-J(W.S.)

= PG

= CO

PATCHWORK KNOW-HOW

These instructions are intended for the novice quilt maker and do not cover all the techniques used in making patchwork and patchwork quilts. They provide the basic information needed to make the projects in this magazine, along with some useful tips. Try not to become overwhelmed by technique – patchwork is a craft which should be enjoyed.

Preparing the fabric

Prewash all new fabrics before you begin, to ensure that there will be no uneven shrinkage and no bleeding of colors when the quilt is laundered. Press the fabric whilst it is still damp to return crispness to the fabric.

Making templates

Templates are best made from transparent template plastic, which is not only durable, but allows you to see the fabric and select certain motifs. You can also make them from thin, stiff cardboard if template plastic is not available. If you use cardboard, paint the edges of the finished template with nail polish to give it longer life.

Templates for machine-piecing

1 Trace off the actual-sized template provided, either directly on to template plastic, or tracing paper and then stick on to thin cardboard. Use a ruler to help you trace off the straight cutting lines, dotted seam lines and grain lines.

2 Cut out the template using a craft knife, ruler and a self-healing mat.

3 Punch holes in the corners of the template, at each point on the seam line, using a hole punch.

Templates for hand-piecing

• Make a template as described above, but do not trace off the cutting line. Use the dotted seam line as the outer edge of the template.

• This template allows you to draw seam lines directly on to the fabric. The seam allowances can then be cut by eye around the patch.

Cutting the fabric

On the individual instructions for each patchwork, you will find a summary of all the patch shapes used. Always mark and cut out any border and binding strips first, followed by the largest patch shapes and finally the smallest ones, to make the most efficient use of your fabric. The border and binding strips are best cut using a rotary cutter.

Rotary cutting

Rotary cut strips are often cut across the fabric from selvedge to selvedge. With the projects we do, be certain to cut the strips running in the desired direction.

1 Before beginning to cut, press out any folds or creases in the fabric. If you are cutting a large piece of fabric, you will need to fold it several times to fit the cutting mat. Where there is only a single fold, place the fold facing you. If the fabric is too wide to be folded only once, fold it concertina-style until it fits your mat. A small rotary cutter with a sharp blade will cut up to six layers of fabric; a large cutter up to eight layers.

2 To ensure that your cut strips are straight and even, the folds must be placed exactly parallel to the straight edges of the fabric and along a line on the cutting mat.

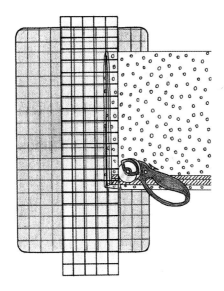

3 Place a plastic ruler over the raw edge of the fabric, overlapping it about ¹/₂ in (1.25cm). Make sure that the ruler is at right angles to both the straight edges and the fold to ensure that you cut along the straight grain. Press down on the ruler and wheel the cutter away from yourself along the edge of the ruler.

4 Open out fabric to check the edge. Don't worry if it is not perfectly straight; a little wiggle will not show when the quilt is stitched together. Re-fold fabric as described in step one, then

place the ruler over the trimmed edge, aligning edge with the markings on the ruler that match the correct strip width. Cut strip along edge of the ruler.

Using templates

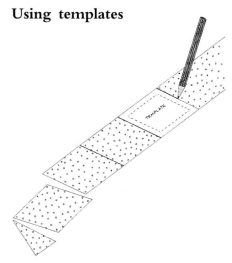

The most efficient way to cut out templates is by first rotary cutting a strip of fabric the width stated for your template and then marking off your templates along the strip, edge to edge at the required angle. This method leaves hardly any waste and gives a random effect to your patches.

A less efficient method is to fussy cut, where the templates are cut individually by placing them on particular motifs or stripes, to create special effects. Although this method is more wasteful it yields very interesting results.

1 Place the template face down on the wrong side of the fabric, with the grain line arrow following the straight grain of the fabric, if indicated. Be careful though – check with your individual instructions, as some instructions may ask you to cut patches on varying grains and some pieces are made up using the wrong side of the fabric as the right side!

2 Hold the template firmly in place and draw around it with a sharp pencil or crayon, marking in the corner dots or seam lines. To save fabric, position patches close together or even touching. Do not worry if outlines positioned on the straight grain when drawn on striped fabrics do not always match the stripes when cut – this will add a degree of visual excitement to the patchwork!

3 Once you have drawn all the pieces needed, you are ready to cut the fabric, with either a rotary cutter and ruler, or a pair of sharp sewing scissors.

Foundation piecing

In paper foundation piecing, the patchwork block design is printed on a piece of paper the exact size of the block. Each part of the block pattern is numbered to indicate the stitching sequence. During the stitching process, the patches are joined together on the paper foundation pattern.

Cutting foundation patches

One of the most important things to remember when cutting foundation patches is that the printed or numbered side of the foundation paper is the wrong side of the block, so you must cut them with the wrong side facing up. Cut a patch for each of the numbered areas on the foundation pattern block, approximately the size and shape of the individual pattern piece shapes, allowing about $\frac{1}{2}$ in (1.25cm) for seam allowances. It is better to cut the patches larger than necessary, as excess is trimmed away.

Arranging cut patches

• Quilt instructions always give you a layout showing how to arrange the various patch shapes to form the overall geometrical design. It is possible to simply stitch the cut patches together at random, but you will often create a much better effect if you plan the design first.

• Lay the patches out on the floor or stick them to a large flannel or felt-covered board, then stand back to study the effect. If you are not happy, swap the patches around until you reach the desired effect.

Basic hand and machine-piecing

Patches can be joined together by hand or machine. Machine stitching is quicker, but hand assembly allows you to carry your patches around with you and work on them in every spare moment. The choice is yours. For techniques that are new to you, practise on scrap pieces of fabric until you feel confident.

Machine-piecing

Follow the quilt instructions for the order in which to piece the individual patchwork blocks and then assemble the blocks together in rows.

1 Seam lines are not marked on the fabric, so stitch $\frac{1}{4}$ in (6mm) seams, using the machine needle plate, a $\frac{1}{4}$ in (6mm) machine foot, or tape stuck to the machine as a guide. Pin two patches with right sides together, matching edges. Set your machine at 10-12 stitches per inch (2.5cm) and stitch seams from edge to edge, removing pins as you feed the fabric through the machine.

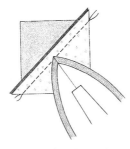

2 Press seams of each patchwork block to one side before joining it to another block, unless doing a Y-seam, then press open.

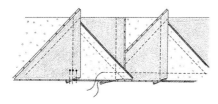

3 When joining rows of blocks, make sure that adjacent seam allowances are pressed in opposite directions to reduce bulk and make matching easier. Pin pieces together directly through the stitch line and to the right and left of the seam. Remove pins as you sew. Continue pressing seams to one side, as you work.

Hand-piecing

1 Pin two patches with right sides together, so that the marked seam lines are facing outwards.

2 Using a single strand of strong thread, secure the corner of a seam line with a couple of back stitches.

3 Sew running stitches along the marked line, working 8-10 stitches per inch (2.5cm) and ending at the opposite seam line corner with a few back

stitches. When hand piecing, never stitch over the seam allowances.

4 Press seams to one side, as in machine piecing, or press them open.

English paper piecing

This is a very easy way to hand assemble a patchwork. Cut paper templates from paper of similar weight to the cover of this book. Do not include the seam allowance in these templates. You will need to cut many accurate templates. Cut the fabric patches roughly $\frac{1}{2}$ in (1.25cm) bigger all around than the template. Place the paper templates onto the wrong side of the fabric. Fold the edges of the fabric over the paper, and using large stitches, baste it to the paper. When you have lots of these patches prepared, attach them to each other by holding the pieces with right sides together and doing a tiny whipstitch along the edge (see glossary). The paper can be removed from a patch after it has been attached at all four sides. The papers can be reused over and over until they wrinkle.

Inset seams

In some patchwork layouts a patch will have to be sewn into a corner formed by two other patches. Use the following method whether you are machine or hand piecing. Do not be intimidated. This is not hard to do once you have learned a couple of techniques.

1 Stitch two patches together, starting at the edges of one very pointed end of the diamond and finishing at the middle dots by one shallow point of the diamond. Reverse stitching at end of stitch line to secure. Press seam open.

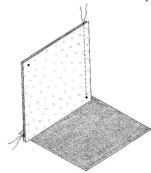

2 First, align the third, or inset patch along one side of the 'V' shape with right sides together and points matching.

Pin pieces together, matching up the middle dots exactly. Stitch this patch in place along the 1/4in (6mm) seam line starting at the edges of the very pointed end, and working down to the middle dot. Reverse stitching at end of stitch line only, to secure. Press seam open.

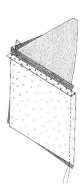

3 Pivot the third, or inset patch, aligning its adjacent side to the opposite side of the 'V' shape. Starting exactly at the middle dot, stitch along the 1/4in (6mm) seam line to the edge of the opposite very pointed end of the diamond. Reverse stitching at the beginning only, to secure. Press seam open.

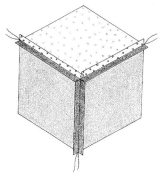

4 Alternatively steps 2 and 3 can be done in one motion. Start step 2 and when you reach the middle dot make sure your needle is down through the fabric. At this point, lift the presser foot and pivot the third, or inset patch as described in step 3. Continue stitching along the seam to the edge of the opposite very pointed end of the diamond.

Foundation piecing

The printed side of a foundation paper is the wrong side of a block, so make sure that the fabric patches are cut with the wrong side up. This is also the side that you stitch from.

1 Set your sewing machine stitch to 18-20 stitches per 1in (2.5cm) and use a 90/14 needle. Use the combination of a large needle and small stitch which will perforate the paper as you stitch, making

it easier to tear away when you have finished.

2 Place the fabric patch that corresponds to the area no. 1 under the pattern with the wrong side of the fabric to the wrong, or unprinted side of the pattern. Pin the two together, making sure that the fabric patch covers the area and overlaps the seam lines on all sides by at least 1/4 in (6mm).

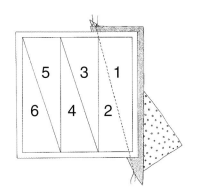

3 Next, place patch no. 2 under fabric patch no. 1, with right sides together and raw edges overlapping beyond the seam line edge. Pin the patch in position. With paper side uppermost, stitch along the seam line marked between no. 1 and no. 2, starting and finishing at the fabric edges. There is no need to reverse stitch the end of each stitch line, as the seams will be secured when the overlapping seams are stitched.

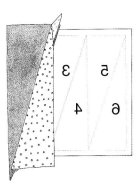

4 Trim the seam allowances to approximately 1/4 in (6mm). Then open out patch no. 2 and press the seam to one side with a hot iron, but no steam as this will make the paper wrinkle.

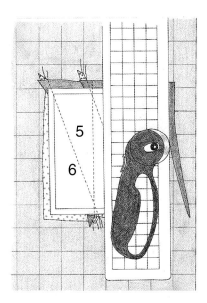

5 Continue to add patches in this fashion, following the sequence on the block. After the last patch has been stitched in place, trim away the excess fabric from around the edge of the block with a rotary cutter and ruler, LEAVING THE DESIGNATED SEAM ALLOWANCE around the outer edge.

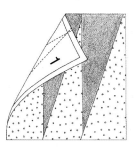

6 Leave the paper foundation on the block until all the blocks have been stitched together. Once all the blocks are joined, tear away the paper.

Quilting and finishing

When you have finished piecing your patchwork and added any borders, press it carefully. It is now ready to be quilted and finished.

Preparing the backing and batting

• Remove the selvedges and piece together the backing fabric to form a backing at least 3in (7.5cm) larger all around than the patchwork top. There is no need to allow quite so much around the edges when working on a smaller project, such as a bag.

• For quilting choose a fairly thin batting, preferably pure cotton, to give your quilt a flat appearance. If your batting has been rolled up, unroll it and let it rest before cutting it to the same size as the backing.

Basting the layers together

1 On a bare floor or large work surface, lay out the backing with wrong side uppermost. Use weights along the edges to keep it taut.

2 Lay the batting onto the backing and smooth it out gently. Next, lay the patchwork top, right side up, on top of the batting and smooth gently until there are no wrinkles. Pin at the corners and at the mid points of each side, close to the edges.

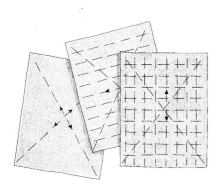

3 Beginning at the center, baste diagonal lines outwards to the corners, making your stitches about 3in (7.5cm) long. Then, again starting at the center, baste horizontal and vertical lines out to the edges. Continue basting until you have basted a grid of lines about 4in (10cm) apart over the entire quilt.

4 For speed, when machine quilting, some quilters prefer to baste their quilt sandwich layers together using rust-proof safety pins, spaced at 4in (10cm) intervals over the entire quilt.

Hand quilting

This is best done with the quilt mounted on a quilting frame or hoop, but as long as you have basted the quilt well, a frame is not necessary.

With the quilt top facing upwards, begin at the center of the quilt and make even running stitches following the design. It is more important to make even stitches on both sides of the quilt than to make small ones. Start and finish your stitching with back stitches and bury the ends of your threads in the batting.

Machine quilting

• For a flat looking quilt, always use a walking foot for straight lines, and a darning foot for free-motion quilting.

• It is best to start your quilting at the center of the quilt and work out towards the borders, doing the straight quilting lines first, followed by the free-motion quilting.

• Make it easier for yourself by handling the quilt properly. Roll up the excess quilt neatly to fit under your sewing machine arm, and use a table or chair to support the weight of the quilt that hangs down the other side.

Preparing to bind the edges

Once you have quilted or tied your quilt sandwich together, remove all the basting stitches. Then, baste around the outer edge of the quilt 1/4 in (6mm) from the edge of the top patchwork layer. Trim the back and batting to the edge of the patchwork and straighten the edge of the patchwork if necessary.

Making the binding

1 Cut bias or straight grain strips the width required for your binding, making sure the grainline is running the correct way on your straight grain strips. Cut enough strips until you have the required length to go around the edge of your quilt.

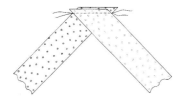

2 To join strips together, the two ends that are to be joined must be cut at a 45 degree angle, as above. Stitch right sides together, trim turnings and press seams open.

Binding quilt edges

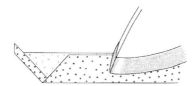

1 Cut the starting end of the binding strip at a 45 degree angle, fold a 1/4 in (6mm) turning onto the wrong side along the cut edge and press in place. With the wrong sides together, fold the strip in half lengthwise, keeping raw edges level and press.

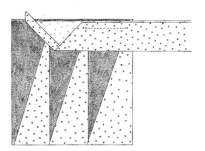

2 Starting at the center of one of the long edges, place the doubled binding onto the right side of the quilt keeping raw edges level. Stitch the binding in place, starting 1/4 in (6mm) in from the diagonal folded edge (see above), reverse stitching to secure and working 1/4 in (6mm) in from the edge of the quilt towards the first corner of the quilt. Stop 1/4 in (6mm) in from the corner and work a few reverse stitches.

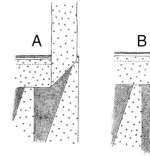

3 Fold the loose end of the binding up, making a 45-degree angle (see A). Keeping the diagonal fold in place, fold the binding back down, aligning the raw edges with the next side of the quilt. Starting at the point where the last stitch ended, stitch down the next side (see B).

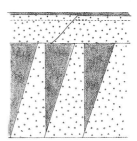

4 Continue to stitch the binding in place around all the quilt edges in this way, tucking the finishing end of the binding inside the diagonal starting section (see above).

5 Turn the folded edge of the binding on to the back of the quilt. Hand stitch the folded edge in place just

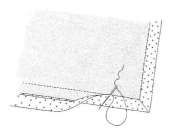

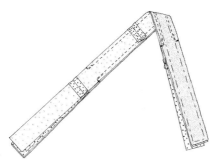

covering binding machine stitches, and folding a mitre at each corner.

Completing the bag

Note: use a $^3/_8$in (1cm) seam allowance throughout, and stitch seams with right sides together, unless otherwise stated.

1 Stitch 4 strap and gusset pieces together to form a long strip, alternating the fabrics and stripe directions along the length. Repeat with the remaining strap and gusset pieces. Press seams open.

2 Stitch the two strap batting pieces together to form a long strip, by overlapping the short ends by $^3/_8$in (1cm) and stitching across. Baste the joined batting to the wrong side of one strap and gusset piece.

3 To form the strap section, baste the two strap and gusset pieces together matching seams and stitching for 15$^3/_4$in (40cm) each side of the center seam along both raw edges (see above). Stitch pieces together along basted edges. Reverse

stitching at each end of stitchlines to secure. Remove basting stitches and carefully snip into the seam allowances at both ends of both stitching lines. Turn through to right side and lightly press.

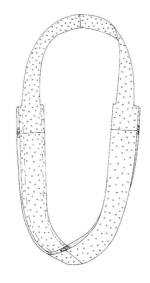

4 Stitch the short ends of the gusset sections together to form a ring (see above). Press seams open.

5 Baste the remaining 2 gusset sections together along the raw edges, then work 5 straight quilting rows of stitching spaced evenly apart between the seam alowances all the way around the strap and the gusset.

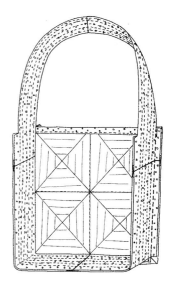

6 Baste the gusset section to the 3 raw edges of both bag sides. Keeping the bound top edges of the bag sides level with the beginning of the strap, match the lower gusset seam with the center seams on the patchwork blocks and snip into the gusset seam allowances to help you turn the bottom corners. Stitch pieces together. Neaten the raw seam edges inside the bag with the binding pieces (see page 46).

GLOSSARY OF TERMS

Backing The bottom layer of a *quilt sandwich*. It is made of fabric pieced to the size of the quilt top with the addition of about 3in (7.5cm) all around to allow for quilting take-up.

Basting Also known as tacking in Great Britain. This is a means of holding two fabric layers or the layers of a *quilt sandwich* together temporarily with large hand stitches, or pins.

Batting Also known as wadding in Great Britain. Batting is the middle layer, or *padding* in a quilt. It can be made of cotton, wool, silk or synthetic fibers.

Bias The diagonal *grain* of a fabric. This is the direction which has the most give or stretch, making it ideal for bindings, especially on curved edges.

Binding A narrow strip of fabric used to finish off the edges of quilts or projects; it can be cut on the straight *grain* of a fabric or on the *bias*.

Block A single design unit that when stitched together with other blocks creates the quilt top. It is most often a square, hexagon, or rectangle, but it can be any shape. It can be pieced or plain.

Border A frame of fabric stitched to the outer edges of the quilt top. Borders can be narrow or wide, pieced or plain. As well as making the quilt larger, they unify the overall design and draw attention to the central area.

Butted corner A corner finished by stitching *border* strips together at right angles to each other.

Cutting mat Designed for use with a *rotary cutter*, it is made from a special 'self-healing' material that keeps your cutting blade sharp. Cutting mats come in various sizes and are usually marked with a grid to help you line up the edges of fabric and cut out larger pieces.

Darning foot This is a specialist sewing machine foot that is used in *free-motion* quilting – the *feed dogs* are disengaged so that stitches can be worked in varying lengths and directions.

Ditch quilting Also known as *quilting-in-the-ditch* or *stitch-in-the-ditch*. The quilting stitches are worked along the actual seam lines to give a *pieced quilt* texture. This is a particularly good technique for beginners as the stitches cannot be seen – only their effect.

English paper piecing An easy hand method of piecing a patchwork together. With this method you baste each patch to an individual paper template, folding the seam allowances onto the wrong side. The patches, still mounted on the paper, are then stitched together before the paper is removed.

Feed dogs The part of a sewing machine located within the *needle plate* which rhythmically moves up and down to help move the fabric along while sewing.

Foundation pattern A printed base the exact size of a *block* onto which patchwork pieces are sewn. The foundations are usually made from soft paper, but they could also be lightweight fabric or interfacing.

Free-motion quilting Curved wavy quilting lines stitched in a random manner. Stitching diagrams are often given for you to follow as a loose guide.

Fussy cutting This is when a template is placed on a particular motif, or stripe, to obtain interesting effects. This method is not as efficient as strip cutting, but yields very interesting results.

Grain The direction in which the threads run in a woven fabric. In a vertical direction it is called the lengthwise grain, which has very little stretch. The horizontal direction, or crosswise grain is slightly stretchy, but diagonally the fabric has a lot of stretch. This grain is called the *bias*. Wherever possible the grain of a fabric should run in the same direction on a quilt *block* and *borders*.

Inset seams, **Setting-in or Y-seams** A patchwork technique whereby one patch is stitched into a 'V' shape formed by the joining of two other patches.

Mitred corners A corner finished by folding and stitching binding strips at a 45-degree angle.

Needle plate The metal plate on a sewing machine, through which the needle passes via a hole to the lower part of the machine. They are often marked with lines at 1/4in (5mm) intervals, to use as stitching guides.

Padding Also known as *batting* in the United States and *wadding* in Great Britain, this is the middle layer of a *quilt sandwich*. Padding can be made of cotton, wool, silk or synthetic fibers and can be bought in sheets or as a loose stuffing.

Patch A small, shaped piece of fabric used in the making of a *patchwork* pattern.

Patchwork The technique of stitching small pieces of fabric (*patches*) together to create a larger piece of fabric, usually forming a design.

Pieced quilt A quilt composed of *patches*.

Pins Use good quality pins. Do not use thick, burred or rusted pins which will leave holes or marks. Long pins with glass or plastic heads are easier to use when pinning though thick fabrics. Safety pins (size 2) can be used to 'pin-baste' the quilt layers together.

Quilting Traditionally done by hand with running stitches, but for speed modern quilts are stitched by machine. The stitches are sewn through the top, *padding* and *backing* to hold the three layers together. Quilting stitches are usually worked in some form of design, but they can be random.

Quilting foot See *walking foot*.

Quilting frame A free-standing wooden frame in which the quilt layers are fixed for the entire quilting process. Provides the most even surface for quilting.

Quilting hoop Consists of two wooden circular or oval rings with a screw adjuster on the outer ring. It stabilises the quilt layers, helping to create an even tension.

Quilt sandwich Three layers of fabric: a decorative top, a middle lining or *padding*, and a *backing*. Collectively these are known as a 'quilt sandwich'. They are held together with quilting stitches or ties.

Rotary cutter A sharp circular blade attached to a handle for quick, accurate cutting. It is a device that can be used to cut up to six layers of fabric at one time. It needs to be used in conjunction with a 'self-healing' *cutting mat* and a thick plastic ruler.

Rotary ruler A thick, clear plastic ruler printed with lines that are exactly 1/4in (6mm) apart. Sometimes they also have diagonal lines printed on, indicating 45 and 60-degree angles. A rotary ruler is used as a guide when cutting out fabric pieces using a *rotary cutter*.

Selvedges Also known as *selvages*, these are the firmly woven edges down each side of a fabric length. Selvedges should be trimmed off before cutting out your fabric, as they are more liable to shrink when the fabric is washed. They are also difficult to quilt due to the firm nature of the weave.

Setting-in See *inset seams*.

Stitch-in-the-ditch See *ditch quilting*.

Threads 100 percent cotton or cotton-covered polyester is best for hand and machine piecing. Choose a color that matches your fabric. When sewing different colors and patterns together, choose a medium to light neutral color, such as gray or ecru. For both hand and machine quilting it helps to use coated or pre-waxed quilting thread, which allows the thread to glide through the quilt layers. Hand quilting can also be worked in special threads, such as pearl or crochet cotton.

Template A pattern piece used as a guide for marking and cutting out fabric *patches*. Usually made from plastic or strong card that can be reused many times.

Tying A quick and easy way to hold the *quilt sandwich* layers together without using machine or hand *quilting*. Thread or yarn is inserted through the quilt layers at regular intervals and tied in a knot or bow, or secured with buttons.

Wadding The British term for *batting*, or *padding*.

Walking foot Also known as a *quilting foot*, this special sewing machine foot has dual feed control. It is very helpful when quilting, as the fabric layers are fed evenly from the top and below, reducing the risk of slippage and puckering.

Whipstitch These are small, even hand stitches used to join two finished edges as, for example, when attaching patches together in *English paper piecing*. The patches are placed right sides facing, with neatened edges level. Insert a needle close to the edge at right angles from the back through to the front, picking up only a few threads. Draw thread through. Continue in this manner, keeping stitches uniform in size and spacing until edges are joined together.

Y-seams See *inset seams*.

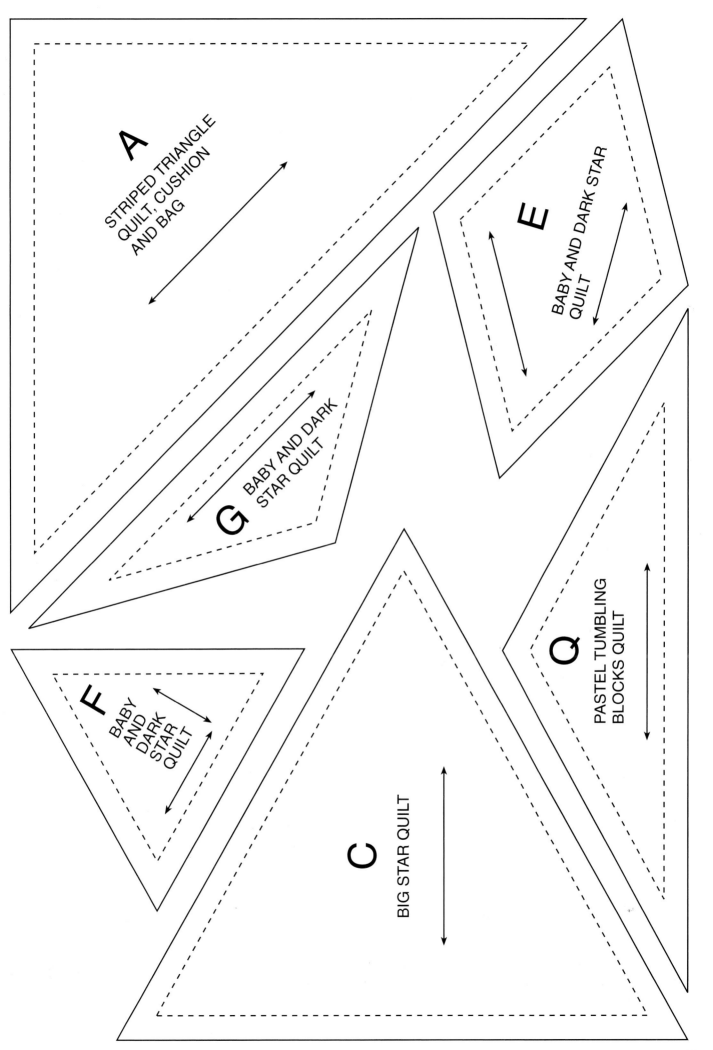

A
STRIPED TRIANGLE
QUILT, CUSHION
AND BAG

E
BABY AND DARK STAR
QUILT

G
BABY AND DARK
STAR QUILT

F
BABY
AND
DARK
STAR
QUILT

Q
PASTEL TUMBLING
BLOCKS QUILT

C
BIG STAR QUILT

49

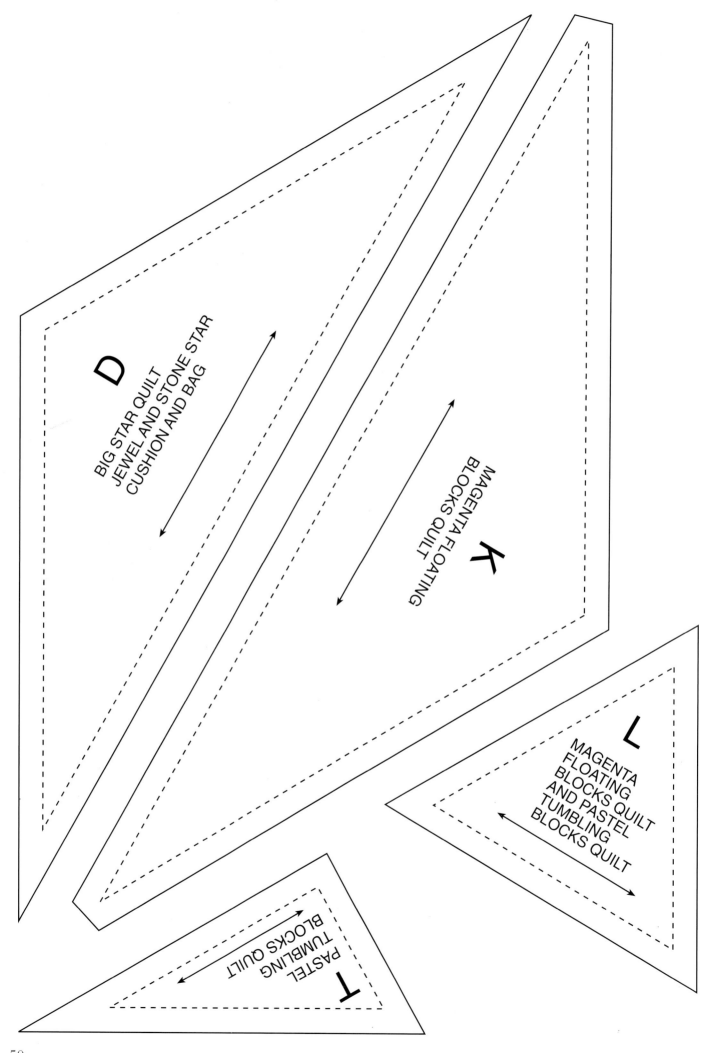

D

BIG STAR QUILT
JEWEL AND STONE STAR
CUSHION AND BAG

K

MAGENTA FLOATING
BLOCKS QUILT

L

MAGENTA
FLOATING
BLOCKS QUILT
AND PASTEL
TUMBLING
BLOCKS QUILT

T

PASTEL
TUMBLING
BLOCKS QUILT

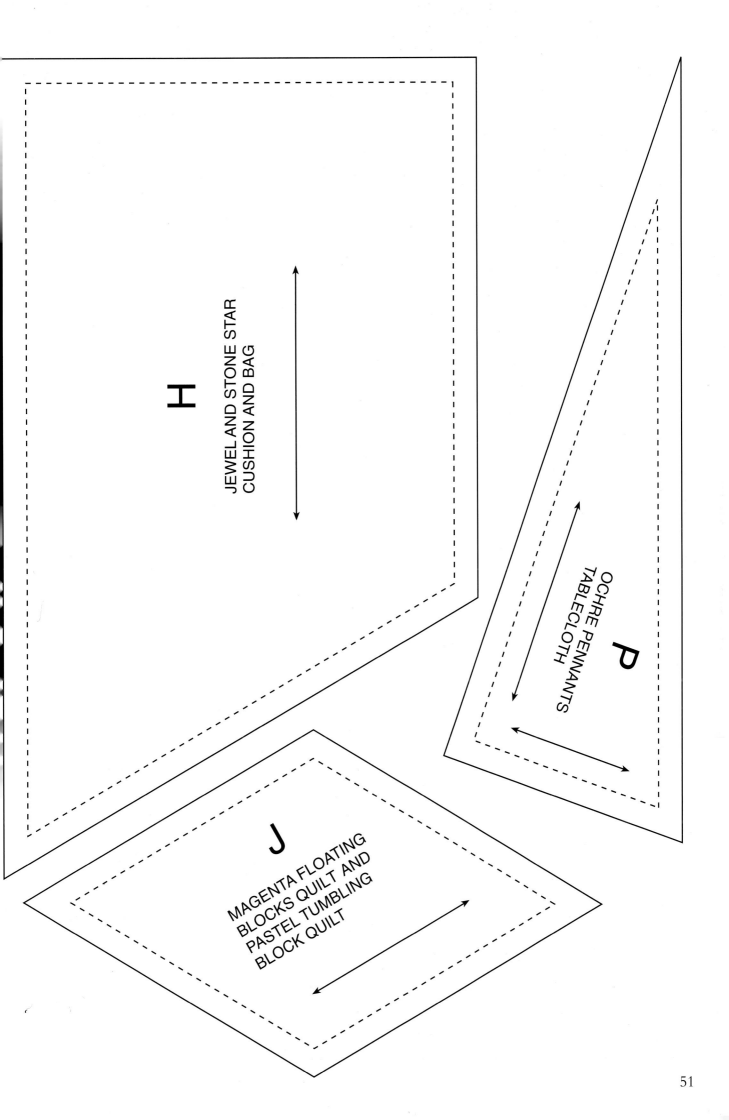

H

JEWEL AND STONE STAR
CUSHION AND BAG

P

OCHRE PENNANTS
TABLECLOTH

J

MAGENTA FLOATING
BLOCKS QUILT AND
PASTEL TUMBLING
BLOCK QUILT

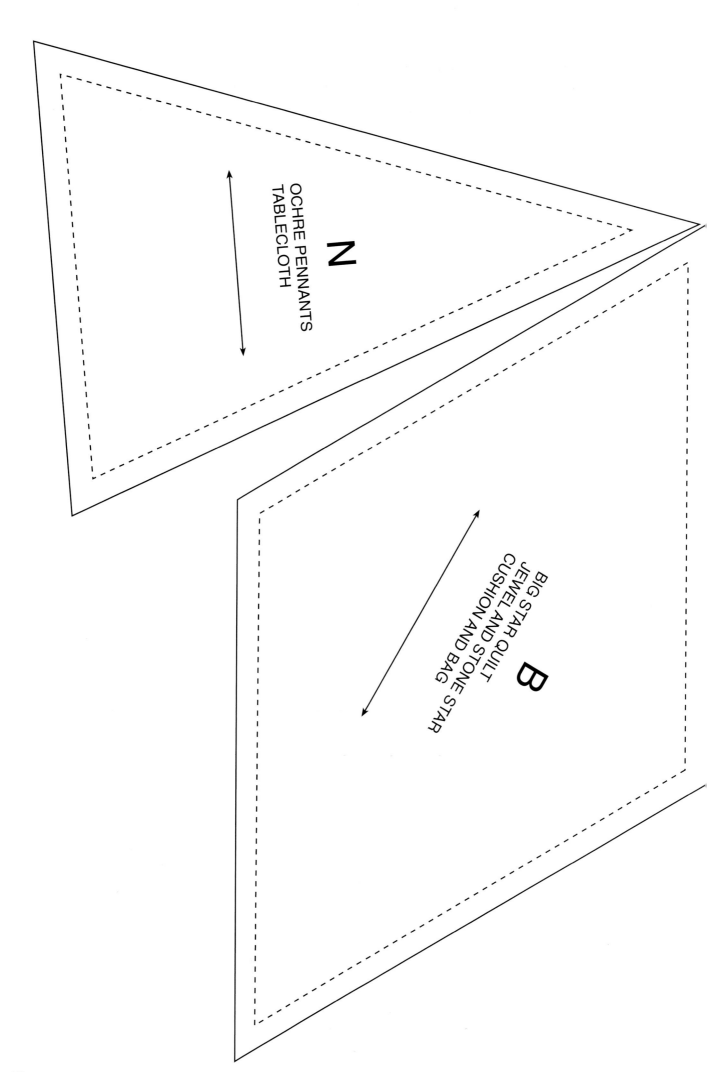

OCHRE PENNANTS
TABLECLOTH

N

BIG STAR QUILT
JEWEL AND STONE
CUSHION AND BAG STAR

B

52

OCHRE PENNANTS FOUNDATION BLOCK

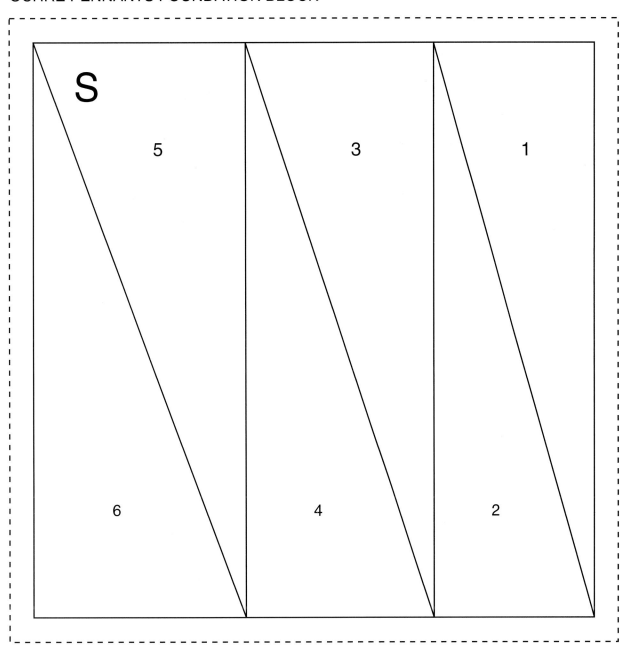

S

5

3

1

6

4

2

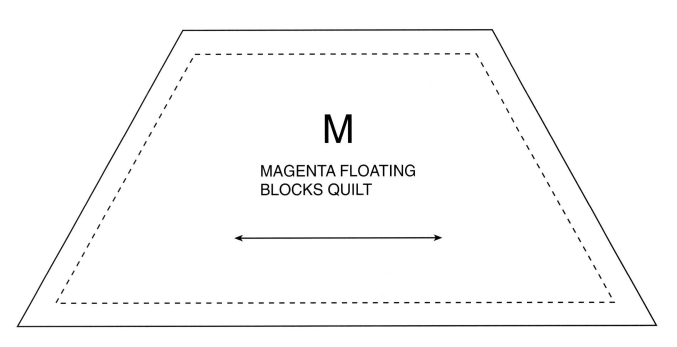

M

MAGENTA FLOATING
BLOCKS QUILT

OCHRE PENNANTS REVERSE FOUNDATION BLOCK

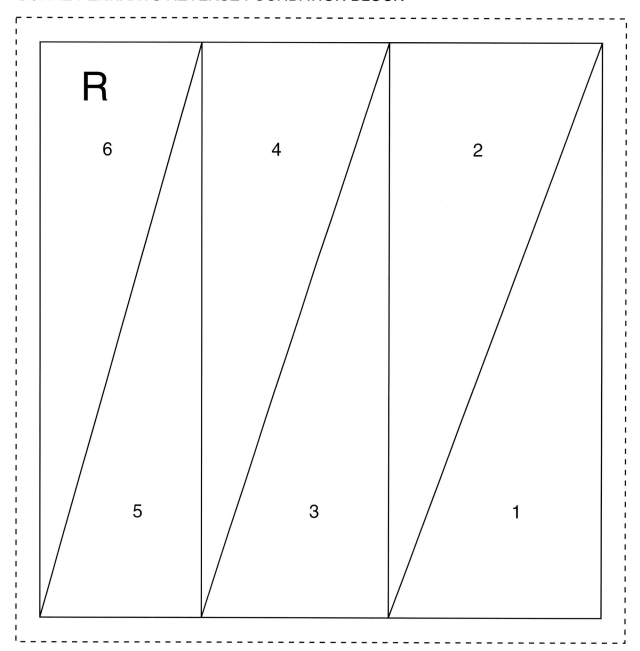

INDEX

Baby Star Quilt   21, 28-30, 49
backing   45, 47
bag   **25**, 47, **35**
bag sides, quilting   25
basting   45, 46, 47
batting   45, 46, 47, 48
bias   47, 48
Big Star Quilt   21, 26-8, 50, 52
binding   23, 46, 47
block   **23**, **28**, **30**, **37**, 47, 48
border   47
Botany wool   28
butted corner   *see* corner

corner
    butted   47
    mitred   48
cushion   21, 24, 29, 33-4, **35**,50, 51, 52
cutter, rotary   43, 47, 48
cutting
    fussy   30, 48
    strip   48
    see also cutter
cutting fabric   43
cutting foundation patches   44
cutting mat   47, 48

Dark Star Quilt   21, 31-3, 49
darning foot   46, 47

English paper piecing   44, 48
experience ratings   21

feed dogs   47, 48
finishing   45-7
foot   *see* darning foot; walking foot
foundation patches   44, 45
foundation pattern   38, 44, 45, 48
foundation piecing   44, 45

grain   39, 47, 48
gusset pieces, bag   47

hand-piecing   44

Jewel and Stone Star
    bag   21, 34-5, 50, 51, 52
    cushion   21, 33-4, 50, 51, 52

Kaffe Fassett Fabrics
    Alternate stripe   21: AS01   22, 23;
        AS10   22, 23, 24, 31, 36, 37;
        AS21   22, 23, 24, 38

Beads   21: GP04-L   41; GP04-C   29,
    41; GP04-P   41
Broad stripe   21: BS01   22, 24, 25,
    31, 36, 37, 38, 39; BS06   22, 24,
    25, 36, 37; BS11   36, 37,
    38; BS23   36, 37
Chard   21: GP09-L   26, 27; GP09-J
    26, 27, 31, 33, 34; GP09-S   26, 27,
    33, 34; GP09-C   26, 27, 29, 30, 41;
    GP09-P   26, 27, 29, 30, 41
Exotic stripe   21: ES01   36, 37; ES04
    26, 27, 36, 37; ES10   31, 36, 38,
    39; ES15   31; ES20   26, 27, 38,
    39; ES21   36, 37; ES23   31, 38, 39
Gazania   21: GP03-L   29, 30; GP03-J
    31; GP03-S   29, 30, 41; GP03-P
    29, 30, 41
Narrow stripe   21: NS01   22, 23, 24,
    25, 36, 38, 39; NS09   22, 23, 24,
    25, 31, 36, 37; NS16   36, 38, 39;
    NS17   31, 36, 37
Pachrangi stripe   21: PS01   31; PS04
    36, 38; PS08   36, 37, 38, 39; PS13
    31; PS14   38, 39; PS15   31
Pebble Beach   21: GP06-L   29; GP06-J
    29, 41; GP06-S   29, 41; GP06-C
    29, 41; GP06-P   29, 41;
Roman Glass   21: GP01-L   29; GP01-J
    31, 33; GP01-S   26, 27, 29, 33, 34;
    GP01-C   29; GP01-P   29, 41

machine-piecing   44
machine presser foot   22
Magenta Floating Blocks Quilt   21, 35-
    7, 50, 51, 53

needle plate   48

Ochre Pennants Tablecloth   21, 38-40,
    51, 52, 53, 54

padding   47, 48
Pastel Tumbling Blocks Quilt   21, 40-2,
    49, 50, 51
patch   48
patchwork   48
piecing   *see* English paper; foundation;
    hand; machine
pins   48
preparing fabric   43
presser foot
pressing   22, 43, 44, 45

quilt assembly   **23**, **27**, **29**, **32**, **36**, **42**
quilting   **37**, 48, 45-7
    ditch   23, 41, 47
    free-motion   47, 48
    hand   46
    machine   46
    see also piecing
quilting foot   *see* walking foot
quilting frame   46, 48
quilting hoop   46, 48
quilting-in-the-ditch   *see* quilting: ditch
quilt sandwich   47, 48

ruler, rotary   43, 48

seam, inset (Y-seams)   37, 44-5, 48
seam lines   44, 45
selvedge (or selvage)   45, 48
setting-in seams   *see* seams, inset
stitch-in-the-ditch   *see* quilting: ditch
stitching: evenness of   46; finishing   46;
    hand   46-7; machine   47; running
44; setting for   45; spiral   33
straps, bag   47
Striped Triangle Quilt   21, 22-3, 49
    bag   21, 25, 49
    cushion   21, 24, 49

tablecloth   38-40, **39**
tacking   *see* basting
template   48: A   22, 24, 25, 49; B   26,
    27, 32, 35, 43, 52; C   26, 27, 32,
    49; D   26, 27, 32, 34, 35, 50; E
    30, 31, 32, 33, 49; F   30, 31, 32,
    33, 49; G   30, 31, 32, 33, 49; H
    34, 35, 51; J   37, 41, 51; K   37,
    50; L   37, 41, 50; M   37, 53; N
    38, 39, 52; P   38, 39, 51; Q   41,
    49; R   54; S   53; T   41, 50
    for English paper-piecing   44
    for hand-piecing   43
    for machine-piecing   43
    making   43
    plastic   43
    using   43-4
ties   *see* tying
tying   48

wadding   *see* batting; padding
walking foot   46, 48
whipstitch   48

Y-seams   *see* seams, inset